FOLLOW YOUR HEART

The Story of Stephanie Bruce's Not-So-Final Season

By Ben Rosario and Stephanie Bruce

Foreword by Three-Time Olympic Gold Medalist
Tianna Madison

Copyright © 2023 by Ben Rosario and Stephanie Bruce

All rights reserved. No part of this book may be reproduced, scanned, or distributed in any printed or electronic form without permission.

Printed in the United States of America
ISBN: 9798375665849

Photo Credits:
Cover: Johnny Zhang
Page 22: Paul Ward
Page 108: Michael Scott
Page 206: Amanda Cortese
Page 224: HOKA
Page 246: Johnny Zhang

Dedication

To my late cousin, Amy Niedringhaus-Johnson, the first person I reached out to when Steph received her congenital heart defect diagnosis in October of 2021. Despite being in and out of the hospital during that time as she awaited a heart transplant, she took the time to respond and then reached out to Steph herself. Amy passed away in January of 2023 and I will miss her a lot.
-Ben

To all those who are scared to follow their heart, who think they always need someone to call, or ask for advice, or ask for direction. That was my mom for me, for my whole life, until a year before this Grit finale journey, that we lost her. Mom, I had so many questions after you died on how my life and my running journey should continue. But after experiencing 2022 on my own, with my own decisions, I know you simply would have told me one thing, "Follow your heart." And that's exactly what I did. And I hope many of you reading follow yours, wherever it may take you.
-Stephanie

CONTENTS

FOREWORD		7
INTRODUCTION	Scrubbing Toilets in Eugene	13
CHAPTER 0.0	The Cast	23
CHAPTER 1.0	Full Circle	55
CHAPTER 2.0	Everything Worked Out Perfectly	63
CHAPTER 3.0	Sisters	71
CHAPTER 4.0	Happy Birthday Ben B	81
CHAPTER 4.5	The Ingebrigtsen Factor	97
CHAPTER 5.0	We Finally Did It Mom	109
CHAPTER 6.0	Aliphine's Back	125
CHAPTER 6.5	Bicuspid Aortic Valve Disease	137
CHAPTER 7.0	Solid Gold	149
CHAPTER 8.0	I'm Relishing the Solo Suffering	161
CHAPTER 9.0	Hurricane Aliphine	171
CHAPTER 10.0	Last Big Day	183
CHAPTER 11.0	Tapering	197
CHAPTER 12.0	Grit Finale	207
CHAPTER 13.0	The Race	225
EPILOGUE	The Decision	247

FOREWORD

Stephanie Bruce is a force. If you are lucky enough to be pulled into her orbit—and I do mean pulled—you must expect that your life will soon change. Not because she demands it of you, but because you're inspired to. Steph and I became friends after a brief exchange of messages on Instagram that led to an awkward FaceTime call. We sat in uncomfortable silence wondering how we, two adult women in a pandemic, were to begin a new friendship. It was Stephanie who broke the ice by asking me excitedly if I wanted to see her notebook of "big ideas." I perked up immediately, "Of course!" I all but shouted, "I have a notebook of ideas too!" Jostling phones that were precariously mounted in front of us we scurried away to grab the notebooks. By the time we returned to our phones we were friends. Because in the time it took for me to bound across the room to retrieve a notebook that I rarely ever let people see, I realized that someone who can make me feel so excited and so hopeful about an idea I had not yet shared was someone I needed in my life.

I am a track and field athlete that specializes in short sprints and the long jump. I was relatively clueless about the world of distance running, in fact 400 meters is long distance to me. I watch Steph with awe. It's not just that she can do dozens of 400s after running 10 miles, or that she has the mental fortitude to stay in a race at mile 24 even as it hurts, even as she can see that the goal she has set for herself is out of reach. It's the other things, it's how she shows up as a wife to Ben, the type of mother she is to Riley and Hudson, how she does not put anything in her body that harms her, can paint her nails on the go, run several businesses, and almost never misses a workout. I may be a two-time Olympian with three Olympic Gold medals but when I think of Steph I think, "Damn, it cannot get better than that."

But she disagrees. So she keeps going. Because even if she's at her best she still wants to know if she can be THEE best. And so I log on at ungodly hours to watch races and tweet my reactions. I repost to support and brag about my friend, and wear all my Grit gear proudly.

For elite athletes like her, who've been doing it for as long as she has, balance is a myth. We often have to sacrifice time spent nurturing certain parts of ourselves in order to give present goals the intense focus they require. And yet, Steph finds a way to not drop those balls and to not let any part of herself feel neglected or unseen. She makes her friends and followers feel the same. She sees herself clearly and helps us see ourselves clearly too. When she called me to "think out loud" about whether this was her last season and her loose plan for the next few years I remember telling her that, "she had nothing left to prove." But I immediately had a flashback to New York City, where we had been just a short few months before, supporting her at the TCS New York City Marathon. All of us were together in her suite, she was in silk pajamas trying to process the race, trying to accept the love all of us wanted to shower her with, trying to eat the burger, trying to smile. I saw an athlete that left her heart *and* legs on the streets of New York, but most importantly I saw an athlete that was *not* finished. I whispered to our friend Sara, "She's not done, watch."

There comes a point in an athlete's life where we wonder if our commitment, discipline, and dedication has become a delusional pursuit of something that was not meant for us. I know that sometimes Steph wonders that about herself, about how many times she can be so close to the dream that she can nearly touch it before she should find a new dream. And yes, even though after each race she debriefs us in a way that leaves us all hopeful and inspired, the heart does break with each disappointment.

Speaking of Steph's heart, the recent loss of Steph's mom was an inflection point in this story. Bravely, she brought us along that journey of navigating grief as it comes, and doing your best to find your way after being shaken. We can all relate to the experience of loss and the profound disorientation that often accompanies it. Still, Steph continued to show up for herself, her family, her training partners, and her fans.

As a woman in sport, society typically views us through the lens of a ticking clock. Whether it's the so-called biological clock ticking, the sands of father time, or in Steph's case the inevitable failure of a heart with a congenital birth defect, Steph does not take time for granted. Not on a stopwatch and definitely not in her life. That's why we're here. I hope through this story you see my friend as I do. As a woman who knows what's in her heart, who is not afraid to share her heart with you, who is unafraid to show you the pieces when it's broken, and will gladly pour into you when it's full. Most importantly, Steph continues to show us that you can change your mind and change your dream, but the one thing you should never change is your desire to follow your heart.

~Tianna Madison
Proud Friend of Steph Bruce
Author of Survive & Advance
2x Olympian
3x Olympic Gold Medalist
3x World Champion
World Record Holder

INTRODUCTION

SCRUBBING TOILETS IN EUGENE

I first met Stephanie Rothstein sometime in the spring of 2012. My wife Jen and I, and our then one-year-old daughter Addison, had moved to Flagstaff that March with very little in the way of a plan. After spending the previous six years as the co-owner of a running specialty store in my hometown of Saint Louis, I was totally burnt out and needed a wholesale change. I had stayed in Flagstaff for three weeks back in 2007 when I was training for the 2008 Olympic Trials Marathon (held in the fall of 2007 in New York City) and immediately fell in love with the town, as most people do. The crisp, cool autumn mornings, the clean mountain air, and the quaint little downtown had an intoxicating effect on me. I had always wanted to come back.

Steph was preparing for the 2012 Olympic Track and Field Trials when I arrived. She and her then fiancé Ben Bruce were part of the adidas McMillan Elite professional running team—founded and coached by Greg McMillan. I had very briefly been a part of the team as well, when it first started, but was coached by Greg remotely. He and I had remained friends and I took a job as marketing director for his online coaching business, McMillan Running Company, when I moved to Flagstaff. His two ventures were mostly separate however, so though I saw a few workouts here and there, and met the athletes, I wasn't really involved with the team. Thus, I can't quite say I recall getting to know Steph all that well right away.

At that time, though Steph was certainly having a very good career—she had run a 2:29 marathon, made a World Half Marathon team, and was becoming a staple near the front of U.S. road races—it was Ben who was the better known of the two. He was one of the top steeplechasers in the country, had finished second at the National Championships in that event in 2010, competed for the U.S. at the 2011 World Championships, and was a favorite to make the Olympic team that summer. In sports, as in life, however, things do not always go as planned.

The 2012 Olympic Trials were held in Eugene, Oregon at historic Hayward Field on the campus of the University of Oregon. That school, and that city, had long been synonymous with track and field in the United States. Distance running, especially, held a special place in the Eugene sports consciousness with names like Bill Bowerman, Bill Dellinger, and the late great Steve Prefontaine having turned the Oregon Ducks into a powerhouse in the 1960s and 70s. Even the sport's most powerful shoe company, Nike, got its start in Eugene when a former Duck named Phil Knight worked with his coach (Bowerman) to create soles using nothing but plain old black rubber and a waffle iron in the coach's kitchen. A few years later Nike signed its first athlete ambassador, Steve Prefontaine. Steph and Ben were no strangers to Eugene. Steph moved there in 2007 shortly after graduating college, hoping to kickstart a professional running career with the Oregon Track Club where she was first coached by the legendary Frank Gagliano. "Gags" was an amazing middle distance coach, leading countless athletes to the Olympic Games in events from the 800 to the 5,000 meters. Ben remained in San Luis Obispo through 2008 with his college coach—1988 Olympic Trials Marathon champ Mark Conover. For Steph, a natural at the longer distances, it wasn't the best fit. She stayed in Eugene but moved on from the OTC while Ben joined the club in 2009 and would eventually begin working with its new head coach, Mark Rowland, a 1988 British Olympic bronze medalist in guess what event—the steeplechase. It couldn't have been a better situation for Ben.

Steph, however, struggled to make ends meet. She took odd jobs where she could, even nannying and cleaning houses (which let's be honest means she was scrubbing toilets) to pay her rent. Things weren't all bad though. She struck up a close friendship with a fellow athlete named Lauren Fleshman who had been an NCAA star at Stanford and was now one of the top runners for the OTC. Lauren and her husband Jesse Thomas, and Steph and Ben, became inseparable. Lauren even helped Steph try and figure out what the heck was going on with her body—why she was having so many digestion issues, why she was so fatigued, and why she just couldn't compete at the level it seemed she was capable of. It was that collaboration between Steph and Lauren that led to doctors diagnosing Steph with celiac disease—a chronic digestive and immune disorder that damages the small intestine.

Because Steph had celiac she couldn't eat any foods that contained gluten. In fact, there are a whole host of foods and ingredients that Steph, and so many others with her condition, have to avoid. But because Steph was an athlete, she needed to fuel her body with healthy food. Much like Knight and Bowerman some 40-plus years before, Steph and Lauren began experimenting in their kitchen to come up with a solution to a problem. They started making easily digestible snacks using natural foods that were safe for anyone with a gluten allergy or celiac disease, and that were tasty enough for anyone, period. They called them, Picky Bars.[1]

In the midst of this whirlwind of a life that included cleaning toilets and founding an energy bar company, Steph remained committed to becoming a true professional runner. It was during this period that she began working with a new coach, Brad Hudson. Brad, another former Oregon Duck, had made a name for himself by running a 2:13 marathon at the age of 24 in 1990—unheard of for an American at that age, in that era. After watching Steph run a 10k road race, and analyzing her form, Brad simply

---

[1] Steph, Lauren, and Jesse went into business together as the co-founders of Picky Bars in 2010. Jesse served as CEO with Lauren as the main recipe creator and Steph as the company's number one ambassador. Picky Bars became a hit with endurance athletes the world over and the company was eventually sold to Laird Superfoods in 2021 for a reported $12 million dollars.

told her, "You're going to be a marathoner." It was a seminal moment for Steph and a conversation that she still recounts to this day.

Now I would love to tell you all about Steph's final year in Eugene, and why she moved to Flagstaff, and why Ben stayed in Eugene at first, and how that affected their relationship, and why he eventually drove through the night to move to Flagstaff, and how he asked her to marry him, and all of the little details that made their life at that time so gosh darn interesting. But I have to save some of that juicy stuff for Steph to tell you herself. She wants to write her own memoir someday and there is no human being that will be able to let you into their soul like Steph. I will be the very first person in line to buy it.

My job here, in this book, is to take you through Steph's final months as a professional runner, and as a marathoner, both of which she did indeed become. Don't worry though, I will make sure to weave plenty of real-life anecdotes (past and present) into these pages, particularly as they relate to her preparation for the 2022 TCS New York City Marathon—the final marathon of her professional career.

I just need to go back to 2012 for a second to wrap up those Olympic Trials in Eugene, and tell you how I got to know Steph personally, and eventually become her coach.

The Trials, held over 11 days from June 21 through July 1, were epic. Rain poured down on the athletes during many of the races, creating some of the more indelible images in the history of Hayward Field. My personal favorite is of Ashton Eaton, on his way to an eventual world record in the decathlon, finishing first in his heat of the 400 meters as his competitors grimace in the background—rain pelting them in the face, while Eaton—in full stride—is simply glancing at the clock. If I was still a kid that would be a poster on my wall.

The men's steeplechase final, though it wasn't raining, was still plenty memorable. Despite experienced athletes like Max King, Billy Nelson, and Ben Bruce being in the field, it was a total newcomer to the event that stole the show. Twenty-three-year-old Evan Jager, who had just tried the steeplechase for the first time earlier that season, ran away from everyone—winning in a time of 8:17.40, more than ten seconds ahead of Ben in fifth and nearly two seconds faster than Ben had ever run in his career.[2] If Brad Hudson telling Steph that she was destined to become a marathoner was a sign of things to come, then the 2012 Trials steeple final was a similar moment for Ben. His chances of ever making the Olympic team in that event—a young man's game—were not looking good. Two months shy of turning 30, his professional running journey, and his life, was about to change.[3]

---

[2] Jager would go on to become the best U.S. steeplechaser of all time, setting the American Record in the event (8:00.45) and winning medals at the 2016 Olympic Games (silver) and the 2017 World Championships (bronze).

[3] Ben would continue competing in the steeplechase all the way until 2017 but never with the same success he had in his 20s. Instead, he transitioned to longer distances—winning five Rock 'n' Roll Marathons in one year in 2014, and became known for his longevity in the sport. His streak of qualifying for, and competing in, 17 straight USA Track and Field Outdoor Championships ended in 2019 and was widely celebrated by the media, fans of the sport, and his competitors.

Depending on how one chooses to spin it, Steph's Trials were a little more promising than Ben's. Coming off a brutally disappointing Olympic Marathon Trials in January, where she had dropped out at 20 miles after never having been a real factor in the race, Steph finished eighth in the 10,000 meters in Eugene. Her time, 32:24.25, was a then personal best—proving that she was getting better with age (a theme that would continue throughout her career) and providing a strong hint that perhaps the best was yet to come.

Steph and Ben were married that fall and would go on to win the women's and men's races at the Big Sur Half Marathon just three weeks later. The framed newspaper article remains displayed in their house to this day.

The following year saw the couple leave the adidas McMillan Elite team with Ben taking over as Steph's coach. And though there were plenty of highlights for Team Bruce in 2013, including Steph's runner-up finish at the USATF 10k Road Championships, it turned out to be a temporary fix.

I got to know Steph and Ben much better during that time. Hard as it may be to believe if you know me now, I even paced Steph in a few workouts in the spring of 2013 while she trained for the Boston Marathon. Steph loves to tell the story of a 12-mile steady state run where, at around 11-and-a-half miles and hanging on for dear life, I blurted out of nowhere, "Where the hell's the finish line?" Whereas Steph has become a better and better runner since that time, I've run less and less and, due in part to a proclivity for Budweiser beer, gained a couple of inches in the old waistline. But I digress.

You can really form a bond with someone when you train hard together. That's one of the things I like most about our sport. You talk on the warmup, and the cool-down, you battle together during the workout itself. As a pacer, the athlete begins to depend on you, and you begin to feel a real sense of responsibility to them. Though I can't remember exact details, knowing what she and I continue to talk about on a regular basis today, I am sure we chatted about the sport at the professional level—how it could be better, and what we could do to help. We are kindred spirits in that way.

When I told Steph that Jen and I had decided to start our own professional team that was set to launch at the beginning of 2014, she was in.[4] So was Ben. That meant an awful lot and gave us instant credibility in the running world. We kept the new name of the team under wraps in the final months of 2013 as we wrote our business plan, and convinced more athletes to join. In addition to Steph and Ben, we gained three other athletes that had previously run for McMillan Elite—Scott Smith, Kellyn Taylor, and Amy Van Alstine. We also had former NCAA All Americans Jordan Chipangama (Northern Arizona), Eric Fernandez (Arkansas), Matt Llano

---

[4] Greg McMillan's team, adidas McMillan Elite, was set to dissolve at the end of 2013. I never intended to start a pro team in Flagstaff but once I found out Greg's team was coming to an end, and since I was coaching a couple of non-sponsored athletes in town with a good amount of success, the idea formed and Jen and I turned it into a reality.

(Richmond), and David Rooney (McNeese St.).[5] It was a pretty darn solid group of athletes and Northern Arizona Elite was born on January 7, 2014.

We were rip, roaring, and ready to go. Except for Steph that is. She was pregnant.[6]

---

[5] I am very proud of the results that original group produced. Matt Llano ran a 1:01:47 half marathon and made the World Half Marathon team for the U.S. Amy Van Alstine won the National Cross Country Championships and represented the U.S. in international competition. Eric Fernandez, who I'd known since he was in high school, finished fourth at the 2016 California International Marathon. Scott Smith spent the rest of his career with us, finished sixth at the 2018 Boston Marathon, and ran a personal best in the marathon of 2:09:46. And then there's Kellyn Taylor who became one of the best U.S. distance runners of her era and at one point had top ten all-time U.S. marks at both 10,000 meters and the marathon.

[6] More about Steph's first two years on the team in Chapter 2.0.

CHAPTER 0.0

THE CAST

I have always viewed each individual marathon training segment as its own story, tailor made for a movie, or a documentary, or in this case…a book. There's a natural narrative arc that begins as the main character, or characters, set out on an epic journey with high hopes, and big dreams, only to run into inevitable tension and conflict along the way in the form of sickness, injury, fatigue, or any of a whole host of real life problems that serve as roadblocks on their yellow brick road to glory. But like in any good script, there's always a climax waiting at the end—in this case in the form of the marathon itself. You can almost hear the dramatic music in your head as race morning plays out, with the athletes nervously bouncing around on the starting line, then standing at attention during the national anthem, and finally leaning forward, hands on their watches, staring straight ahead like caged animals as the gun goes off.

And the best thing of all for me, as the author of this particular tale, is that the whole thing writes itself. There's no need for any Hollywood hyperbole, or bending of the truth, or alternative facts (to use the unfortunate parlance of our times). The highs and lows will be there, I promise, as will the laughter and tears, the moments of ecstasy, and of despair. And all I really have to do is make sure I document them, as they happen, so all of you get the full unabashed version of these next few months. But before I begin, before I dig into the details of each and every week, you need some context. Namely, you need to know the main characters. Thus, this chapter is all about introducing you to the real life human beings who will shape the pages of this book, and help me convey the true emotions of the marathon.

Stephanie Bruce: Steph is our main character. I think we all know that. And a great number of you may think you already know her story because you've followed her for years, watched her interviews, listened to her podcasts, and read her social media posts. And you are probably right. Few professional athletes, across all sports, have shared their journey like Steph. I'm not so pompous as to think that I can tell you more than you already know. But I do hope to chronicle this portion of her life, these final 12 weeks leading into the 2022 NYC Marathon, in a way that brings you even closer to this wonderful person. I'll start with a little bit of history.

Steph, as a child of divorce, moved around a lot—growing up first on the East Coast and then the Southwest. As a senior in high school, Steph took a trip to see her ailing father in New York City as he battled cancer.

Halfway into my senior year my dad's health had been declining–he had been diagnosed with prostate cancer seven years prior. On February 8, 2002 my grandmother died in our home in Phoenix with my mom and brothers surrounding her in the final moments. We flew out to Greensboro, North Carolina for her memorial where my grandfather was buried. From North Carolina I decided to fly out to New York to visit my dad and I remember getting up Saturday morning and I went for a run and I had the strangest feeling on that run; it was very hard to explain what the feeling was because I wasn't necessarily a spiritual person but something was just off, I guess, on that run. When I got back my family friend Dennis told me, 'Your dad passed away' and I said, 'No, I'm actually about to go see him' and he's like, 'No, he passed away in the last hour.' So, I realized that, I think while I was on that run is when he actually died, and so maybe that feeling I had was him kind of passing through me. And yeah, so I guess at a very young age, eighteen years old, it kind of just changed the trajectory of my life. Running shifted from something that I have to do, and it became something I get to do. It almost became a gift to me.[1]

---

[1] Throughout this book I will be sharing quotes directly from Steph. I have not asked her to write anything down. Rather, these quotes are straight from the heart, spoken at the end of each week, to me (except for this one which was taken from a documentary about our team), and recorded on the spot—no second takes, just her raw feelings at the time.

In the summer of 2002, after a fantastic final high school track season that saw her finish second at the Arizona State Championships in the 1600 meters, Steph headed off to begin her collegiate career at the University of California at Santa Barbara.

Her first two years at UCSB were a blast. Steph quickly became one of the leaders on the team, leading the Gauchos to a 1-2-3-4 sweep at the Big West Conference Cross Country Championships as a sophomore. But as her junior year began, things were not so good behind the scenes. Steph's mother Joan was struggling financially. There were plenty of reasons, and no one really to blame, but the bottom line was that there was no money. Not to pay the mortgage on her house, and certainly not to pay for college at UCSB. She had moved into a one-bedroom apartment and her loan application for Steph's tuition was denied.

With debt approaching $40,000, and nowhere else to turn, it appeared Steph was going to have to leave UCSB.

Mark Patton of the Santa Barbara News Press wrote an article in October of 2004 about Steph's situation.[2] Patton quoted Steph, and her coach, Pete Dolan, and her teammate Rebbeca Zamolo.[3] All three talked about the Gauchos' tight-knit group and how far the athletes had come in just a short time together. Zamolo talked about Steph's leadership, how she was

---

[2] www.ucsbgauchos.com/sports/w-xc/spec-rel/103104aaa.html

[3] Like Steph, Zamolo has built a loyal following on social media with 3.2 million followers on Instagram: @rebeccazamalo

the one everyone went to for advice, and how the team wouldn't have made it to Nationals without her. Dolan talked glowingly about Steph the athlete and the person, but also about how, as a parent, he wouldn't want his child to leave college with $100,000 in debt. As such, he said he would understand if she had to transfer.[4]

Not long after the article was released, a still-to-this-day anonymous donor read it and paid for the remainder of Steph's education in its entirety. She would go on to lead UCSB to a ninth-place finish at the 2006 NCAA Cross Country Championships, and twice finish as an All American in the 10,000 meters on the track. To this day, Steph holds the school record in that event and no Gauchos cross country team, men or women, has ever finished as high as her 2006 squad at NCAAs.

Those two transformative moments in Steph's life—the untimely passing of her father, and the generosity of a stranger, drove her to find out just how good she could be. Upon graduation she moved to Eugene, Oregon, and took jobs nannying and house-cleaning just to get by as she tried her hand at professional running. It was during that time that she found out she had celiac disease, and that its nasty side effects had been holding her back from reaching her full potential. Not only did she change her diet and see immediate positive results, she also used her new understanding of the

---

[4] You might be wondering why a Division I program like UCSB wouldn't just give an athlete like Steph a full scholarship. Well, that's not always how it works. Not all DI programs are what's called, "fully funded," meaning that they do not have as many scholarships available as their counterparts. In order to field a full team, the Gauchos coaching staff had to divide up the scholarships they did have into small chunks, with no athlete able to receive a "full ride."

dietary needs of athletes to create an energy bar company with her friends Lauren Fleshman and Jesse Thomas, a company they sold in 2021 for $12 million dollars.

So let's just say she's come a long way since cleaning toilets in Eugene. In fact, for the last 10-plus years, she's lived in Flagstaff, Arizona where she and her husband Ben are raising their two rambunctious boys, Riley and Hudson, and where Steph has seen a tremendous amount of success in her sport.

She's become an inspiration for runners of all ages and abilities through the transparent sharing of her journey and has publicly announced that 2022 will be her final year as a professional runner. At 38 years old, and recently diagnosed with a congenital heart defect, Steph decided to retire so she and Ben could add to their family and so that she could go out on her own terms. Her fans follow her every move and her final year, her Grit Finale as she calls it, has been Steph's way to make sure that she connects with those fans as much as possible before she runs her last race.

Ben Rosario (Me): I've been just about everything there is to be in the running industry from professional athlete, to event director, to running store owner, to marketing director, to coach, and I currently serve as the executive director of HOKA NAZ Elite. As it relates to this book, however, you should first and foremost think of me as the narrator. I am here to recount the events of these next 12 weeks as they happen, in real time. And like the narrators in *A Christmas Story*, *The Wonder Years*, and *How I Met Your Mother*, I'll throw my own opinion in there along the way.

I have probably dated myself with the previous sentence already but as I write this book I am 42 years old—having spent the last 20 years of my life making my living off of running in some way, shape, or form. Like everyone, though, my childhood had a major impact on the adult I am today. I grew up in a lower middle class neighborhood smack dab in the city of Saint Louis, Missouri where I watched sports, played sports, and loved sports. And when I say I played sports I am not talking about the 2000s suburban version of kids' sports where parents pay a boatload of money for the privilege of driving their kids in the family minivan to an organized practice where everyone sits in line waiting to do the next drill as explained to them by whatever parent got suckered into coaching the team. No. I played streetball and pick-up games more than anything else. And I was competitive. Very competitive.[5]

My mother used to always ask/yell at me, "Why does everything have to be a competition?" To which I suppose my response (which I smartly kept to myself) was, "Because it's way more fun that way."

And so it remains for me to this day. Winning, or to use softer verbiage—meeting challenges, is what drives me in all of my decision making. Most recently, after eight-plus years as both the head coach and executive director of the HOKA NAZ Elite professional running team, I chose to

---

[5] Note that I said competitive, not good. Though I probably spent more hours practicing baseball, basketball, and soccer than any of my buddies, I was never the best kid on the team. However, that all changed when I tried out for cross country in high school and my propensity for practice paid off in a sport that rewarded aerobic response to training as much, or more, than inherent skill.

hand over the coaching reins to two-time Olympian Alan Culpepper in the spring of 2022 so I could focus on my director duties. I felt that in order for us to meet the challenge of becoming the best team in the country we needed a head coach who could focus exclusively on training and on the athletes, and a director who could focus exclusively on advancing the team's brand from the business and marketing side of things.

I couldn't be happier with the decision and writing this book is actually just an amplified version of one of my main duties—athlete storytelling. We cannot expect fans to be excited about the performances of our athletes unless they feel like they are a part of the process along the way. I believe that wholeheartedly. Because though I was a communications major with an emphasis in journalism, I think my fanatic sports viewing habits from the time I was five years old provided me with an honorary degree in sports marketing—one that I've been able to put to good use for the last two decades in the running industry.

You'll hear a little bit more about me as this whole story unfolds, but you can definitely expect that I'll be involved in Steph's training and coaching in this, her final season. As Alan himself said, "It would be foolish to abandon something that's been working so well."

Ben Bruce: Ben (aka Ben B) is no doubt going to be a central figure in this story. You might say he'll be one actor playing many roles. As Steph's husband he is her biggest supporter, her biggest fan, and at times—her cook. As the official NAZ Elite pacer, he is often her workout partner—responsible for ensuring that she hits the right splits on workouts that sometimes cover as much as 20 miles in length. That's a long time for a husband and wife to be running together. But they love every minute of it. I don't know if jealous is the right word, but I certainly admire Ben and Steph's marriage. It's not a knock on my own of course, but theirs is a marriage that just seems to be such a fairytale. Ben and Steph first met at the 2005 NCAA Outdoor Track and Field Championships where he was running the steeplechase and she was running the 10,000. A mutual friend, J.T. Service, introduced the two of them—a fact he likes to remind the Bruces of to this day.[6]

Their first date was like so many first dates across the world…awkward.[7] Steph pulled into Ben's neighborhood in San Luis Obispo and searched for the right house. Unfortunately, she didn't find it. She walked slowly up to the neighbor's house, right across the street, and nervously knocked on the door.

"Is Ben here?," she asked.

"No, he lives across the street."

Ben watched the whole thing from his front window, amused. When Steph finally made her way to the correct abode, Ben asked her if she was hungry. She said yes, thinking that maybe he'd be taking her to lunch

---

[6] J.T. is the owner of Soul Focus Sports, a highly successful event management company in the endurance space.

[7] Steph's full recap of this date in Chapter 4.0.

somewhere in beautiful downtown San Luis Obispo. Instead, he marched straight into the kitchen and fixed her up a tuna sandwich. If you know Ben you know that it's not necessarily that he wouldn't have liked a nice lunch, but if there was tuna in the fridge, he wasn't going to let it go to waste for pete's sake. The man is inherently frugal.[8] Of course, they couldn't have known it then, sitting at that kitchen table eating a tuna sandwich, but through a decade of entrepreneurial endeavors that the couple has taken on together, Ben's frugality has been the perfect yin to Steph's yang. And they certainly couldn't have known that they'd fall in love, get married, have kids, and be just as in love at nearly 40 years old, and after nearly ten years of marriage, as any couple you'll ever meet.

I hope to do justice to Ben and who he is as a husband, a dad, and a person in the telling of this story over these 12 weeks. I am sure his super dad skills will be in full effect, especially as Steph gets nearer and nearer to NYC. His boys really couldn't have a better father. Ben puts his endless energy to good use by coaching their baseball and soccer teams. And he puts his inner child to good use as well, serving as another playmate in countless backyard games of catch and cornhole, and just general mayhem.

There is not a person on this planet that I've met who was more naturally suited to be the dad of two boys, and the husband of a professional athlete, than Ben Bruce.

Aliphine Tuliamuk: Aliphine (aka Allie or Allie T) is one of Steph's

---

[8] A trait passed down from his father, Paul.

teammates, and a very close friend. The two of them, along with Kellyn Taylor, have run thousands of miles together and been part of the core of our team since 2018. That's when Aliphine joined the squad, although because she's been such a great fit it seems like she's been around since the beginning. When she visited Flagstaff to see if joining our team was the right move for her (and vice versa), I distinctly remember being blown away by her personality much more than anything else. She has this contagious smile and laugh, and way of communicating, that sheds positivity on anyone within shouting distance. I knew that she was super talented; she was ninth at the World Junior Cross Country Championships when she was just 15 years old and had already won seven national titles before she became a member of NAZ Elite, but I remember thinking how shameful it was that her previous shoe sponsor hadn't amplified her brand.[9] She was a star with an incredible backstory, and I wanted the whole running world to hear it.

Aliphine was born in a small village in Kenya, one of 32 siblings. Yes—32! She lived a completely rural upbringing, void of nearly all the modern amenities we've become accustomed to in the U.S. And yet, sight unseen and the first in her family to do so, she had the ambition to come to this country to attend college...in Iowa of all places. She later transferred to Wichita St., became a 14-time All American, and then decided to stay in the U.S. and try to make it as a professional runner. After struggling to

---

[9] To be eligible for the World Junior Championships an athlete must be under 20 years of age, and not turning 20 until after the year in which the competition takes place. Thus, at 15, Aliphine beat all but eight of the athletes in a field of the best 19-and-under distance runners in the entire world.

make ends meet running road races and picking up a few thousand dollars here and there, she eventually signed a shoe contract that allowed her to stay in the country she had grown to love. In 2016, after a multi-year process, she finally became an American citizen. Four years after that, Aliphine won the Olympic Trials Marathon in dramatic fashion and represented her new country in the Tokyo Olympics. She's now married with a beautiful one-year old baby girl—the living embodiment of the American dream.

As far as her role in this book, it will hopefully be a big one. Like Steph, Aliphine will also be running the NYC Marathon. The two of them will overlap in training a good bit but not for every single workout. We have always valued group training at NAZ Elite, but never at the expense of individual needs. In the last year or so Steph has thrived on very controlled training and incorporating "double workout" days into her schedule.[10] Aliphine has continued to excel off of the style of training we used to prepare for the 2020 Olympic Trials so her segment will likely include more of the "monster" sessions we've been using at NAZ Elite for the last

---

[10] Double workout days are not brand new, but they've gained a lot of popularity in the professional running world after the success of Norway's Jakob Ingebrigtsen—the 2021 Olympic Champion at 1500 meters—who incorporates these double days year-round. They involve a very controlled workout in the morning—often at marathon-type effort, and then another very controlled workout in the evening—often at a slightly faster effort. You'll see these workouts described in detail as Steph executes them in training.

eight-plus years.[11] If Aliphine can get to the same level of fitness she achieved going into those Trials, then it is my belief she will have a legitimate chance to win in New York.

Alan Culpepper: Alan is a two-time Olympian having represented the United States in the 2000 Games in Sydney in the 10,000 meters, and the 2004 Games in Athens in the marathon—where he finished 12th. Of course, he's much more than that, but I feel obligated as a former journalism major to go all inverted pyramid style on you when given the opportunity to throw the term Olympian out there. Plus, it's become sort of a habit lately as part of my job has been to promote Alan's hiring and say to the running world that this guy is going to bring us to a whole new level. The nice thing is, I really believe it.

When I sat down with Mike McManus, HOKA's global director of sports marketing, in the spring of 2021 to talk about that summer's recruiting class, Mike was very keen on adding some 1500 meter and 5,000 meter

---

[11] The whole philosophy behind "double workout" days is, over the course of time, to maximize the time spent in certain key training zones. Some of the workouts that NAZ Elite has implemented over the years subscribe to this same philosophy but they accomplish it in one session. Workouts like 20 x 1-kilometer, 15 x 1-mile, or 5 x 2-miles at half marathon-marathon effort allow the athletes to spend 10-15 miles in these important zones but force them to do so on tired legs (late in the workout). This simulates the feeling those athletes will have late in a marathon, a feeling that is necessary to achieve/master in practice should one expect to be able to deal with it on marathon race day.

specialists to the team.[12] He mentioned a number of names until I stopped him and said, "That sounds great, and I'm all for it, but we'd need to bring in another coach because that's just not my specialty."

Mike paused and then said, "We could do that."

So there it was. For all intents and purposes, our search for a new head coach started that day. Looking back, I'd have to say that it was a tad chaotic at first. We made a list of the very top coaches in the NCAA, thinking originally that a huge key was going to be hiring someone that could boast a big-time record working with college athletes and producing national championships in those desired events on the track. We ended up receiving legitimate interest from four of the five coaches on our original list, and conducted a number of Zoom calls that summer and into the fall. For non-disclosure reasons I cannot share the names of those candidates, or the one candidate who we really fell in love with during that time. All I can say is that it didn't work out, and by winter break we were back to the drawing board and had pivoted to looking for a coach who could not only appeal to 1,500 and 5,000 meter runners but who had experience all the way up to the marathon. It had become clear to me by that time that I was going to need to spend way more time on the business and marketing side

---

[12] In the world of professional running, there is no draft like in the NBA, MLB, or NFL. All of the athletes are essentially free agents, able to choose wherever they'd like to run and with what shoe company and/or team they'd like to sign. So in that way it's much more like the college recruiting process. We analyze all the seniors who'll be completing their eligibility, decide who we think could be a good fit for NAZ Elite, and we recruit them—starting with phone calls and emails, then a visit, and if all goes well...a contract offer.

than I ever had before in order for us to keep up in what was becoming an increasingly competitive marketplace.[13]

One of the "outside the box" candidates we had thought about in the fall, and spoke with, was Alan. We knew that after trying his hand at a number of business endeavors once his own athletic career had ended, he was itching to get back into the world of professional running...specifically he wanted to start his own professional training group.[14] He had actually reached out to Mike about that very subject before he knew anything about our search. He and Mike knew each other from Mike's days at adidas

---

[13] Perhaps due at least in part to our success at NAZ Elite, shoe companies have begun to realize that sponsoring an entire team provides a much larger return on investment than sponsoring individual athletes here and there. Teams like the Hansons Brooks Distance Project in Michigan, and the Nike Bowerman Track Club in Portland, had been thriving even before NAZ came around. But more recently, structured and well-funded groups began popping up all over the place. New Balance has a group coached by Mark Coogan in Boston. adidas got back in the game big time—sponsoring a group coached by Terrence Mahon in San Diego in addition to their support of the Boston Athletic Association team, the Atlanta Track Club, and Tinman Elite. Reebok launched a group coached by Chris Fox in Virginia. Puma started a team in North Carolina headed by Alistair and Amy Cragg. And perhaps the biggest disrupter of the whole bunch has been what's called the On Athletics Club (OAC) in Boulder, Colo. headed up by Olympian Dathan Ritzenhein. The OAC had unprecedented success right out of the gate, putting multiple athletes on the 2021 Olympic Team. They were the group that truthfully made my decision quite easy. Alan can go up against Dathan. I'll take on their marketing team. Let the games begin!

[14] Like me, Alan has worn a number of different hats, including, also like me, founding, owning, and eventually selling his own running store—Solepepper Sports. Some of his other adventures included commentary work for major road races, working for The Competitor Group where he became vice president and race director for the Rock 'n' Roll Marathon Series, and a job with the University of Colorado where he served as director of operations and marketing for their Conference on World Affairs.

where he worked in sports marketing and Alan was an adidas-sponsored athlete. Knowing he had that desire put him on our radar, but he lacked one big thing we were looking for—experience at the college level.

Luckily for us, Alan's mind was very much made up about what he wanted to do with the rest of his life. He wanted to coach. So much so that he took a job that fall at the University of Texas El Paso as the cross country coach and assistant track coach. With a wife and four kids, this is not a decision he made lightly. Of course, it helped that his better half, Shayne, was an Olympian herself—having competed for the U.S. at the same two Olympics as Alan, but in the 1,500 and the 5,000. No one could truly understand his passion for the sport like Shayne. There was a problem though; Shayne and their three youngest children (their oldest, Cruz, was already in college), would be staying in Boulder, Colo. while Alan commuted back and forth from El Paso. It wasn't an easy situation, but when Mike and I reached back out to Alan around Christmas it showed us just how committed he was to his new profession.

I remember that Zoom call well. And what I remember was one line above all others. At one point, unsolicited and in the course of conversation, Alan said, "If you guys hire me you're going to look like geniuses."

It was such a powerful line but uttered so naturally, and with such confidence, from a man who is otherwise quite humble. I was pretty darn close to being sold right then and there. But it was after his visit to Flagstaff that spring when it became crystal clear that Alan was our guy.

He and I hit it off as if we'd known each other for ten years.[15] But more importantly, he won over the athletes. And that included the veterans.

Steph texted me after she met with him and said very simply, "You should hire Alan."

We did. And I hope that Alan taking over as head coach, and working with Steph in her final season, can be an entertaining subplot throughout this story.

Jenna Wrieden: Jenna has been a part of what we do at NAZ Elite since January of 2021. She is our assistant coach, a position we decided to add after Ben Bruce—who had served as a part-time assistant in 2019 and 2020 as he transitioned away from his own professional running career, decided that his family obligations would not allow him to take on a full-time role. With a growing team, and with me serving as both coach and director, we really needed a full-time assistant as 2021 approached. But we couldn't just hire anyone so we opened up a full-on search, posting the job on social media and asking for applications from anywhere and everywhere.

NAZ Elite operates as a 501c3 non-profit organization which means we have a Board of Directors to answer to on major decisions, like the assistant coaching search. I was certainly glad to have our Board as we went through the entire process. Right off the bat we established a couple of important things. Number one was we wanted to stay open-minded,

---

[15] I had never met Alan before all of this.

meaning that the job search was wide open. We did not want to limit ourselves by saying the candidates had to have college or pro coaching experience, for example. We were absolutely open to the idea that a high school coach could be the right person. In fact, experience, in general, wasn't a caveat. We were not opposed to a young adult, with the right energy and attitude, coming in and taking on this role. The whole idea behind being open to anything was driven by the fact that we had never had a full-time assistant coach before and so who were we to say what we needed? We wanted to give everyone a chance, and believed that the right candidate would reveal themselves during the course of the process, naturally. Basically, we didn't want to craft the perfect assistant coach in our mind and then try to find someone to fit that mold. We wanted to allow the perfect person to show us what it was that we needed.

And number two, and this is important, we were not going to hire a female just so we could say, "Look at us, we hired a woman for a coaching job." My wife Jen, and Pamela MacMahon, the two females on our Board, were very adamant about that from the get go. So with no limitations on this thing, we set off to find NAZ's assistant coach in the fall of 2021. We ended up receiving more than 80 applications from all walks of life. We did indeed have a good number of high school coaches apply, as well as rookie coaches in their 20s, and veteran coaches in their 60s. Some folks even applied with no coaching experience at all. I ended up conducting more than 30 interviews before we finally narrowed it down to our final three candidates. We brought each of the three finalists to Flagstaff on separate visits, so they could hang out with the team, interact with the athletes, spend time with me, etc. And the Board came in handy once again, interviewing each candidate without me present so they could form their own opinions.

I leaned heavily on the opinions of the Board members, as well as on the opinions of the athletes, to make the final decision. I will not share the names of the other two finalists, but I do have to say that they were both amazing. In the end though, Jenna stood out for a number of reasons. For one, she did have a lot of college coaching experience, which we realized as the search went on was going to be necessary to achieve buy-in with our athletes. Jenna had worked at the Division I level at Arizona State University, High Point University, and the University of Louisville. She was the head coach at High Point so it was clear she could lead. But at the same time, as she said to me, she had come to the conclusion that she was more suited for an assistant role. I really appreciated that comment because it told me that—hey—here's a person who's done a lot of self-reflection and knows who they are, and what they do best. That sort of self-awareness was impressive. Probably above all, though, she is just such a caring person. You could tell, even on a short visit, that she was going to be invested in the journey of each and every NAZ Elite athlete, regardless of their personality, and regardless of their performances. She was just very simply going to care…a lot.

Fortunately, we were right. Jenna was hired at the end of 2020, moved to Flagstaff with her husband Nate, and began working for us in January of 2021. In a way, I feel bad because, in retrospect, she came in what turned out to be a weird year—by no fault of her own. But more on that later. And it turned out to be a challenging year for her personally as well, as she told me in the spring that she and Nate were expecting. Though, to be fair, that one was her fault—and Nate's.[16] They welcomed baby Dev into the world in September and Jenna spent the next eight weeks on maternity leave. By that time, we were in the thick of the head coaching search that eventually led us to Alan. I am sure that could not have been an easy thing for her—finding out that she was going to be working with a different head coach than she had signed on for, but she handled it like the total professional that she is.

And now that Dev is one, and Jenna's been here for almost two full years, it really feels like she is a part of the core of who we are. She handles all the daily and weekly communication with the athletes regarding meeting times and locations, workout details, etc. She also designs the team's speed and agility work, as well as the core routines—all things she really enjoys. And she and I still talk a lot about each athlete, and their needs—especially the athletes that were here when she arrived and I was the head coach. Of course, as is the nature of being an assistant coach, you may not hear quite as much about Jenna as you will about some of the other "cast members," but I assure you that when it's all said and done, she'll have been a big part of Steph's final marathon.

Matt Baxter: Matt, like Steph and Aliphine, is scheduled to run the New York City Marathon this fall. I am choosing my words carefully there, and knocking on wood, because he was also scheduled to run New York last year but had to pull out with an injury. Unfortunately, the "I" word has

---

[16] I was joking there in case you didn't pick up on it.

been a big part of his time at NAZ Elite. Matt was an absolute stud during his tenure at Northern Arizona University, helping the Lumberjacks to their first ever national team title in cross country in 2016, and then helping them do it again in 2017 and 2018. That 2017 race was a dominant performance from NAU, and Matt nearly won the individual race as well.[17] He and his teammate Tyler Day pushed the pace from a long way out, essentially daring anyone in the field to go with them, and only one person did (or perhaps only one person could). That was Justyn Knight of Syracuse.[18] With less than a half mile to go, Matt pushed hard, finally gapping Tyler, and placing the favorite, Knight, on the ropes. It was only in the final 150 meters that the speedier Knight finally unleashed his patented kick, eventually getting the best of Matt by less than a second.

After watching that race, I wanted to do everything possible to get both Matt and Tyler on NAZ Elite. Matt's NCAA eligibility was up first, in December of 2018. I put together a pitch for him to look at, I spoke with him face to face, I had some of our athletes write him personal notes…I just wanted him to know that we wanted him, and we wanted him for multiple reasons. Of course he was a high-level athlete, but I knew from talking to his college coaches at NAU that he was also a tremendous teammate and leader. That really appealed to me and his coaches were certainly right—he's been awesome. If there's anything that's been a bummer it's that because of the injuries he hasn't been able to be the

---

[17] https://youtu.be/f7JP1M5q_GE

[18] Knight would go on to compete at the Tokyo Olympics, finishing seventh in the 5,000 meters.

athlete, nor the leader, that I know he can be, and still very much think he will be.

In fact, it might all be coming this segment. As Steph finishes up her time with NAZ, and I think it's safe to say she's been a team leader, perhaps there will be some symmetry as Matt trains alongside her, runs his first marathon while she runs her last, and begins to lead in the same way he did at NAU. Above all, I just hope he can stay healthy. He deserves it after all the hard work he's put in, and I can tell you it's going to be one heck of an emotional moment if and when he crosses that finish line in Central Park on November 5.

Kellyn Taylor: If Steph has been the heart of the team over these last eight-plus years, then Kellyn has been its soul—crushing workouts, showing up and performing to the best of her ability on all of the biggest days, and proving to her teammates that there was more to life than running. During her time with NAZ, in addition to training 100-plus miles a week, and traveling all over the globe to compete against the best in the world, and being the mother of an awesome kid (Kylyn—who was four years old when NAZ began), Kellyn also chose to get her EMT license, study firefighting, and become a foster parent. As I have told Kellyn before, as a coach I haven't always understood her decisions, she makes things harder on herself than she seemingly needs to, but as a human being I have always admired them.

One of our original team members in 2014, Kellyn got better as the team got better. By 2016, she was one of the best female distance runners in the

United States, and had a real shot to make the Olympic team that year in either the marathon, or on the track at 10,000 meters, or both. The Marathon Trials came first, in February, and she was as fit as she'd ever been. I believed she could do it. On a hot, humid day in Los Angeles though, in only her second marathon, she made a rookie mistake. She wasn't patient. She took the lead early on and pressed the pace, a move that broke things up and proved she belonged—it was soon down to only the handful of true contenders, but that ultimately cost her. The mental and physical energy she spent in front, in my opinion, was a waste.[19] Amy Cragg (first) and Shalane Flanagan (third), who had tucked in behind Kellyn for much of the first half of the race would go on to make the Team and Des Linden, who had bided her time in the chase pack, would pick up the pieces over the second half—catching Kellyn, and eventually Flanagan, to finish second. It was the second Olympic team for both Linden and Cragg, and the third for Flanagan. Kellyn would fade all the way to sixth, a massive disappointment internally, even though to the outside observer it may have seemed like a good result. Experience played a role for sure, and as I told Kellyn and all of our fans at a post-race party that night in L.A., we were going to go to Eugene [for the Track Trials that summer] and we were going to make that team.

Before the 10,000 meters at those Trials, I believed Kellyn was going to finish in the top three with every bone in my body. I remember telling her that if she ran to the best of her ability, three people were not going to beat her. Simple as that. I recall getting a text from Lee Cox, head of sales and

---

[19] She has never admitted this. Extreme stubbornness is one of her many traits.

marketing for HOKA at the time, right before the race that read, "This is it." We all believed. But sports are cruel sometimes. You can believe. You can do everything right. You can perform to the best of your ability…and you can still lose. Kellyn finished fourth. It was crushing.

As I remember it, it was sometime after that race that Kellyn began adding things to her plate. The armchair psychologist in me wonders if taking on some of these extra challenges was a sort of coping mechanism to deal with the devastating feelings she experienced in 2016, putting every ounce of herself into those Trials races, and coming away empty-handed. But to her credit, it's not as if she has ever used any of these extracurriculars as an excuse. Honestly, she never mentions them at all unless asked. In 2017, as she was training for that year's New York City Marathon, she was also going through intense firefighter training—sometimes leaving her back in pain after carrying heavy hoses up and down buildings. She would go on to finish eighth at NYC. In 2018 she was seriously considering trying to get a job as a firefighter in Flagstaff, and yet somehow continue her running career. Quite candidly I did not think this would be possible, but all I could do was ask her to truly think about it and picture all the negatives, not just the positives. In the end, she chose to put her firefighting dreams on hold, but it could have easily gone the other way. A year after that, in 2019, she and her husband Kyle began fostering children—a journey that would cause them more joy, and anguish, than they could have ever imagined. Through it all though, she continued to get even better still as a runner. By the time 2020 rolled around, it was time for another shot at the Olympic Team. At 33 years old, she was in the physical prime of her career. However, fostering was taking a big-time emotional toll. She and Kyle were burning the candle at both ends and sometimes it seemed like she didn't know which end was up. She arrived at one of the very first workouts of the Trials training segment without her racing flats, not realizing that we had a hard session that day. I was pissed. I had never let it bother me that she took on all these other things as long as she showed up and performed, but forgetting about a workout was unacceptable. Things got better after that day in terms of her getting locked into the segment, but life outside of running only got tougher. It all came to a head on January 15, 2020, the day of one of our toughest workouts—15 x 1-mile with 1-minute rest. Unbeknownst to any of us as we drove one hour south of Flagstaff to the tiny town of Camp Verde, Kellyn had had a devastating morning.[20] Without any warning at all, a cab showed up at the Taylor house at 6 a.m. to pick up the two boys they had been fostering for months. Kellyn and Kyle thought these boys were it. They loved them with all their hearts and really believed an adoption was forthcoming. But as often happens in the world of fostering, a relative had decided they wanted the children back, and they get a whole bunch of chances to do so.

Kellyn, Aliphine, and Steph crushed the workout. Together every step of the way, they ran all 15 repeats as fast, or faster, than prescribed—alternating 5:35 and 5:25 to simulate the pace changes they were likely to face in Atlanta. On the cool-down, Kellyn finally broke. She started crying and told Allie and Steph what had happened that morning. Then all three

---

[20] Camp Verde sits at only 3,300 feet above sea level so we often drive down there to do workouts at faster paces than we can run up in Flagstaff. It's especially nice in the winter when Flagstaff is quite cold and temperatures in Camp Verde are up to 20 degrees warmer.

of them started crying, and they hugged, right there on the streets of Camp Verde.[21] There were no teammates on the face of the planet, in any sport, closer than those three, during that segment.

Somehow, Kellyn stayed mentally focused on the task at hand, but physically it was all too much. Two weeks out from the race she felt a pain in her shin that just wouldn't go away. Diagnosed as shin splints, we kept her on flat ground and soft surfaces as the Trials approached so as to not make things any worse. During the race, she felt easy aerobically. Her fitness was as good as it had ever been. But at 20 miles, the pain was too great. She couldn't cover the moves being made and faded to eighth.

Later that week she got an MRI. Turns out she had run 26.2 miles on the hilly streets of Atlanta, against the best runners in the United States, with a stress fracture in her tibia.

As of the writing of this book though, I am happy to say that things are much better for Kellyn, and her family. In the spring of 2022, they finally adopted a little boy named Koen. They are currently fostering a little girl they hope to adopt this fall. And in the middle of all of it, in classic Kellyn fashion, she added one more log to the fire. She and Kyle are pregnant. The (most likely) final Taylor child is due on January 1, 2023—about 13 months before the 2024 Olympic Trials Marathon.

---

[21] A similar hug would occur six-and-a-half weeks later at the finish of the Olympic Trials when all three embraced, crying tears of joy for Aliphine, and of empathy for Steph and Kellyn. The moment was captured on NBC and would go on to win them a Musial Award® for sportsmanship.

The Rest of the Team: Adding Alan to the mix in May allowed us to go into the 2022 recruiting season, guns-a-blazin'. HOKA gave us the green light to spend their money on the top NCAA distance runners in an effort to turn NAZ Elite, eventually, into the best team in the country. I am biased but I think we crushed it. Before we even officially brought Alan on, we signed 2021 NCAA Indoor national champion Wesley Kiptoo of Iowa State. Wesley joined us in March and promptly went out and won the Pittsburgh Half Marathon in a team record—1:01:25. Wesley then helped us land a competitor/friend of his—Adrian Wildschutt of Florida State. Adrian had been the runner-up at the NCAA Cross Country Championships and was the South African record holder in the indoor 5,000 meter run. Having both Wesley and Adrian then made us look a lot more attractive to the third male athlete we signed—NCAA outdoor 5,000 meter champion, Olin Hacker of Wisconsin. Olin is a true track star, with speed that could absolutely put him on a U.S. Olympic team in the future. And he's got the pedigree too. His father, Tim, was an NCAA champion and a USATF national champion.

We did just as well on the women's side, signing NCAA champion Krissy Gear from Arkansas—one of the nation's top 1500 meter runners, and Abby Nichols from Colorado who had run the second-fastest time in the NCAA in the 5,000 during the 2022 season. They joined Katie Wasserman, the runner-up in the 5,000 at the 2021 NCAAs, who we had signed last summer, to form one heck of a young nucleus. We certainly hope that Abby, Katie, and Krissy can enjoy the same sort of success that Aliphine, Kellyn, and Steph have achieved during their many years at NAZ.

All of the young athletes joined not only Aliphine, Kellyn, and Steph, and Matt Baxter—who I've already talked about in this chapter, but a slew of veterans whose credentials and personality give our team a fantastic overall chemistry. Julia Griffey was a soccer player in college that only joined the cross country and track teams at Division II Southern Indiana after the coach saw her running laps around campus as a senior. She ended up as the national runner-up in the 10,000—the second time she had ever run the event. After a journey that saw her move back to her hometown of Saint Louis, get a job in corporate America, and run only for fun at first, she eventually returned to serious competition in her mid 20s. At the 2020 Olympic Trials Marathon she finished a surprising tenth place and signed with NAZ later that year.

Julia's pal Alice Wright is also a marathoner, but with a very different background. An outstanding junior athlete in Great Britain, she chose to come to the United States for college and landed at the University of New Mexico. She excelled for the Lobos, earning eight All-American certificates and four times finished in the top eight at the NCAA Championships over 10,000 meters. An example of stick-to-it-iveness paying off, due to myriad injuries and a global pandemic—Alice did not run a single race in more than two years between July of 2019 and September of 2021. But she came back with a bang and eventually finished second at the 2022 Chevron Houston Marathon, earning her a spot to represent Team Great Britain at the 2022 European Championships Marathon where she finished 22nd.

We hope that Tyler Day and Nick Hauger can take to the marathon in the same way that Alice and Julia have. Nick is off to a good start having made his debut in the event last December when he finished third at the California International Marathon in 2:12:59. He is slated to run CIM again this December, but this year the race will serve as host to the USATF National Championships. A top finish that day could mean a lot for Nick's career and put him in a great position as he looks toward the 2024 U.S. Olympic Marathon Trials. Tyler, meanwhile, has a ways to go after having had Haglund's Deformity surgery last year, followed by a recovery process that has been less than ideal. However, I am confident that he will recover and get back to his old self. His old self being one of the top American prospects to come out of the NCAA in 2020. At the time, he was the U.S. collegiate record holder in the indoor 5,000 meters and was looking at a possible national title in that event before COVID-19 led to the cancellation of the 2020 Championships. I believe that not only will Tyler eventually be a great marathoner, but also that he's versatile enough to compete at a high level across all disciplines. It would not surprise me at all if he were to become a multiple-time national champion. I should also mention that Nick and Tyler are two of the most positive human beings you could ever meet.

Speaking of positivity, the only two athletes I have yet to mention are in that same boat. Lauren Paquette joined us in the winter of 2020 and after a couple of months it seemed like she had been on the team forever. I wish she had actually. She was 33 years old when we signed her, and I have to wonder what it would have been like if she had trained with Steph and Kellyn back in 2014 when we launched NAZ. She responded to altitude, and to the way we train, right away and set a personal best in the 5,000 meters later that summer. Unfortunately, that was the year the pandemic canceled the Olympic Trials. There's a big "what-if" there because the next summer she finished seventh at the Trials, but she was dealing with an injury. Timing is such a big thing in sports so we'll never know what might have been. Looking forward though, things are still very bright for Lauren. She's loving Alan's training, she's healthy, and I am starting to think that the final years of her career, in her mid-to-late 30s, could possibly resemble Steph's. And that would be pretty darn awesome.

Last but not least I have to tell you about Alex Masai. Alex signed with us in the summer of 2021, after a breakout senior season at Hofstra University that saw him set personal bests of 13:24.68 for 5,000 meters and 27:45.19 for 10,000. He ran both of those marks at the NCAA Outdoor Championships, and I was there watching. I drove out to the Airbnb where he and his coach were staying (Alex was the only Hofstra athlete to qualify), and hung out for a bit after the meet. I was all in on this kid right away. He had only finished sixth in that 10,000, but it was how he looked and how he raced that caught my attention. Objectively, no athlete in that race was as smooth as Alex. I welcome anyone to tell me differently. Add to that the fact that Alex didn't even run in high school (he played team handball instead), and that his brother Moses and his sister Linet were both Olympians, and I felt like we were getting a steal.[22] After a year on

---

[22] They weren't just Olympians. Linet was the bronze medalist at the 2008 Olympics in the 10,000 meters and Moses was fourth in the same event on the men's side. The following year, at the World Championships, Linet won gold and Moses won bronze. Alex's brother Dennis was also a professional runner, and his sister Maggie is still running professionally.

the team, I know we got a steal. Alex is uber talented, and a great teammate and person. Like Steph, he takes his job very seriously, and has already become a team leader—arriving at practice early, always, and executing every workout with a surgeon's precision. Plus, he smiles and laughs at every joke anyone makes. It's good to have someone like that around.

I cannot promise every single person on the team will get mentioned in this book, but I assure you that they are all a part of Steph's journey. And when I talk about the vibe of the team, everyone contributes to that. All of Steph's successes over the years have been aided by her teammates in some way, and all of her current teammates are over the moon about what she's accomplishing in her final season. A rising tide raises all boats.

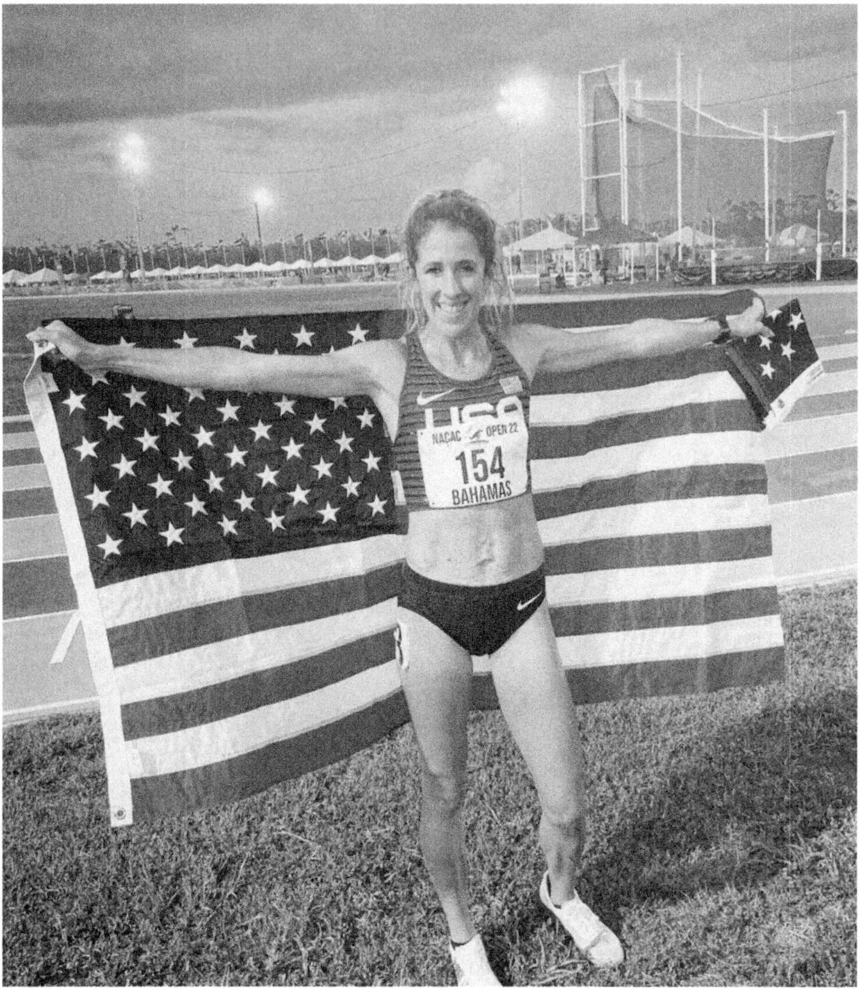
NACAC OPEN 22
154
BAHAMAS

CHAPTER 1.0

Full Circle

12 WEEKS OUT FROM THE NYC MARATHON
AUGUST 15TH – 21ST

The 2006 North American, Central American and Caribbean Athletics Association (NACAC) Championships for Under-23-year-olds was held in the city of Santo Domingo in the Dominican Republic. For United States athletes competing in college, it was a great chance to represent their country, many for the first time, in international competition. Medal winners at the meet in some of the more high profile track and field events like the sprints, hurdles, and middle distances included future Olympians

Dawn Harper Nelson, Natasha Hastings, Leo Manzano, Alysia Montaño, Jason Richardson, and Shannon Rowbury…among others. Meanwhile, winning the women's 10,000 meters was a little known athlete from the University of California at Santa Barbara—Stephanie Rothstein.

When Steph got the call 16 years later that she was being offered a spot to represent her country at the senior NACAC Championships, again in the 10,000 meters, she had to think about it. Harper Nelson, Hastings, Manzano, and Richardson had all gone on to win Olympic Medals, and were all retired. Steph had stuck it out though, and at age 38 was still going strong. However, for reasons we'll get to later, this was it for her as well. She had announced in January that 2022 would be her, "grit finale," the final year of her professional running career—one that had included national titles, World Championship appearances in the half marathon and cross country, top ten finishes at the Chicago, London and New York City Marathons, and despite coming tantalizingly close at the 2020 Marathon Trials—no Olympic appearances.

She had to decide whether or not NACAC would be a good stop on this farewell tour. Earlier in the year she had said yes to seemingly everything (making my job as her coach much harder I must lovingly say) and had run well at the USATF Cross Country Championships, the Rock 'n' Roll Arizona Half Marathon, the NYC Half Marathon, the Boston Marathon, the USA Track and Field (USATF) 10,000 meter championships on the track, and the Mastercard Mini 10k…among others. After the 10,000 meter championships, where she finished seventh against a field in which she was the oldest athlete by three years, and the Mini 10k where she set a massive lifetime best for a road 10k, she wanted to keep it rolling. She decided to enter the Gold Coast Marathon in Australia in search of a PB (personal best) over 26.2 miles. Maybe the running gods decided we were getting too greedy but nothing really went well in the month leading up to Gold Coast. Her energy level was totally off. She was forced to cut workouts short. Her mileage took a hit. Basically nothing pointed to the race going well, and it didn't. Steph ran her slowest time in four years and one of the slowest of her whole career—2:32:22.

After Gold Coast we really had to reassess things and come back to reality. If we wanted to end this year, and her entire career, on a good note we were going to have to make some tough choices on what to say yes to and what to say no to. And those decisions all had to hinge on what was going to be best in terms of preparation for the TCS New York City Marathon on Sunday, November 6. One of the first things we did was limit the racing schedule leading up to New York. Right away she wanted to run the Great Cow Harbor 10k on September 17. Cow Harbor had won the bid to serve as the 2022 USATF Road 10k Championships, an event that Steph's won before when it was in Atlanta in 2018. She got no argument from me on that one. The other options were the USATF 20k Championships in New Haven, Conn. on Labor Day or the Falmouth Road Race in Massachusetts on August 21. New Haven was a little close to Cow Harbor, and Falmouth was potentially too early in the segment to race what would undoubtedly be a very good field. And then she got the call about NACAC.

With this being my last year I just was like, 'Listen I know I didn't make an Olympic team, I know I never made a World track team, and people inside the sport know the levels of what certain teams mean, and I knew that NACAC wasn't necessarily like, 'Oh you're making the Olympic team,' but to me I got to represent the United States one last time in my career and that felt like a privilege.

She was in. And hey—the Bahamas, where the meet was being held, aren't so bad. Well, they aren't so bad for hanging out on the beach. Running 25 laps around a track at roughly five minutes per mile—that's sort of a different story.

The field for the race was small. It looked like Steph's toughest opponent would be her USA teammate Emily Lipari. Steph had finished just two seconds ahead of Lipari at the USATF Championships back in May so we knew they were evenly matched at the distance. However, Lipari had only recently started experimenting with the longer distances. She was better known as a miler. Jenna looked up what Lipari had done since May:

June 11th – Portland Track Festival 1500 – 4:06.0
June 26th – USATF 5,000 meters – 16:15.4
July 9th – Sunset Tour Mile – 4:31.5
July 15th – Sunset Tour 1500 – 4:10.9

Let me be honest with you here folks; Steph Bruce can't run 4:06 for 1500 meters. Nor can she run 4:31 for a mile. Bottom line is we didn't want this thing to come down to a kick. I spoke with Alan, as well as Jenna, and we all decided that running a fairly honest pace from the gun would be the best strategy. However, we had to think about what the heck that meant in a race where the temperatures were going to be in the high 80s with humidity levels above 70%. There are plenty of calculators on the internet where you can plug in a race time, then plug in the temperature, and you'll get a conversion—a new mark equivalent in effort to your goal time but slower due to the conditions. We thought Steph could probably run about 31:40 for 10,000 meters at this point in the season in good weather. The calculator spit out 32:58 (79 seconds per lap) as the equivalent.

Alan took the job of talking about the race with Steph. As part of transitioning him into the head coaching role, and transitioning me out of it, he needs to be the one handling these chats. And though focusing on my executive director role has been smoother than I could have imagined, I will say that I miss both the pre- and post-race talks. I suppose you'd have to ask the athletes but I think I was pretty good at them. Especially the pre-race. It's crazy to think that I've had more than 600 of those talks during my eight-plus years as head coach of NAZ Elite. Anyway, I am sure Alan conveyed the message. And I'm sure Steph agreed. She's no dummy after all. That's one of my favorite things about working with Steph actually; she has incredibly high goals but never strays beyond what's truly physically possible. She lives in what I like to call optimistic reality.

The race did indeed go off in the hot, humid conditions that were predicted. Steph's husband Ben had accompanied her on the trip, and USATF had sent an excellent coaching staff, so she had plenty of people cheering for her—a good thing since the crowd was small. Let's just say the

10,000 meters is not a terribly popular event among the Bahamians. Back in the U.S., I was watching the race on YouTube from a bar in Taos, New Mexico where I was hanging out for the weekend on a "Man Trip" with four of my best friends. I can only imagine what the other patrons were thinking as the five of us huddled around my phone watching a track meet during happy hour.

For the first two miles of the race Steph and Lipari chose to follow Puerto Rico's Beverly Ramos around the track. Ramos, a versatile athlete with personal bests ranging from 2:06 for 800 meters all the way to 2:31 for the marathon, was certainly someone to be respected. After an 83-second eighth lap, however, Steph went to the front and dropped a 79 to get things moving again. Lipari followed and Ramos fell back. It was now a two-woman battle. The next six laps saw Steph and Lipari trade leads with each circuit being run in anywhere between 78 and 81 seconds. Once again, though, it was Steph who put in a surge on lap number 16, running a 77—the fastest of the race to that point, and it was enough to build a small lead. From there on in, Steph kept the pedal down—running each lap in that 77-79 second range as her lead continued to grow. A 75-second final circuit turned out to be a victory lap as much as anything with Steph crossing the line in 33:12.42, a full 42 seconds ahead of Lipari in second.

As Steph said when she made the decision to go, it wasn't the Olympics, but it was still a privilege. And I'll tell you this; winning always feels so gosh darn good.

STEPH'S TRAINING THIS WEEK:

Monday: 10 mile easy run

Tuesday: AM – 3 x 300 with 1-minute rest, 1 x 1600 (cutdown style), 400 jog recovery, 3 x 300 with 1-minute rest
PM – 5 mile easy run

Wednesday: 4 mile easy run

Thursday: 8 mile easy run

Friday: AM – 4 mile easy run
PM – 3.5 mile easy run

Saturday: AM – easy shakeout run
PM – NACAC 10,000 meters. 1st. 33:12.42

Sunday: 4 mile easy run

Total Weekly Mileage: 57.5 miles

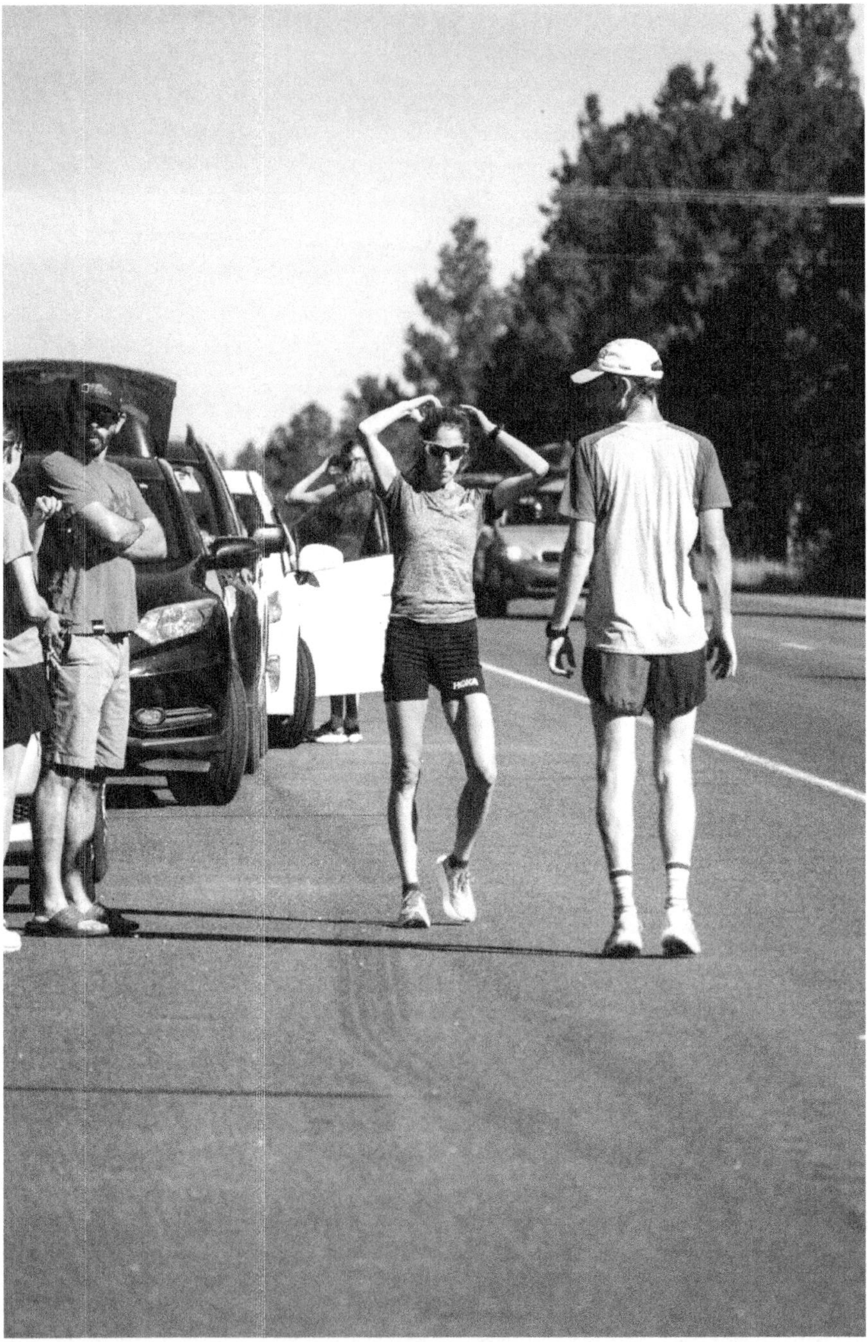

CHAPTER 2.0

Everything Worked Out Perfectly

11 WEEKS OUT FROM THE NYC MARATHON
AUGUST 22ND – 28TH

Coming off a race can be tricky business in the midst of a marathon training segment. Oftentimes the athlete feels quite good energy-wise, especially if it went well, and is riding the high from the weekend and thus wants to keep it rolling. And of course, if it goes bad, they want to get right back to a hard workout to "make up" for the race. Little coaching tip for you: in either situation you have to be the voice of reason. Racing takes a physical and emotional toll on an athlete and that needs to be both acknowledged and respected. The longer the race, and the longer the travel to and from that race, the longer the post-race recovery needs to be.

Steph was coming off the big win on Saturday night in the Bahamas and so we all knew this week was going to be fairly easy training-wise, Steph included. At this stage of her career, she doesn't succumb to many of the mistakes that a younger (or less experienced) athlete might make. Alan and I decided on an easy fartlek on Thursday and a pretty normal long run on Saturday with the last 4-6 miles at marathon effort, but no faster. As is quite organically becoming the case as this segment goes along, Alan wrote the details for the shorter workout, the fartlek, and I wrote the details for the long run. This feels like the natural, and prudent, thing to do since my greatest successes as a coach have come in the marathon and Alan hasn't coached a high-level marathoner since 2007.[1] Having him observe some of the big marathon-specific sessions that I believe have led to so many of our great performances, and then analyze those sessions and determine how they can fit into what he wants to do moving forward, will make our team better in the future. I really believe that.

The biggest challenge for Steph this week wasn't really the workouts, or the mileage, it was life.

---

[1] Alan coached himself throughout the majority of his professional career from 1996 through 2008. As a marathoner, he had two top-five finishes at Boston, a sixth-place finish at Chicago, won the 2004 Olympic Trials, and was 12th at the Olympic Games in Athens. In 2007 he ran his final marathon, a DNF (did not finish) at the Olympic Trials in New York City.

Ben went to UTMB and that was a great gift for him—having HOKA take him out there.[2] That's been a bucket list race and I was so glad he got to experience that. He takes care of our family and does everything. I can handle one week of doing all the things. So for me it was more just normal life stresses, planning my week out. Riley and Hudson, who are six and eight, getting them to school. Getting to practice. It's always a full-time job but it felt like an amplified full-time job.

As if being a temporary single mother of two wasn't enough, Steph had come away from the NACAC race with an unexpected, and unwanted, prize—a blister on her toe that turned into what appeared to be some sort of fungus, and was finally diagnosed as a staph infection. I'll just say it; it was gross. It really bothered her on Thursday's fartlek which was fine in the short term. The workout itself wasn't a big deal in the greater scheme of things, but you never want an athlete to be compensating for anything and I am always worried when something is wrong with the foot. It can be very tempting for the body, subconsciously, to begin landing even imperceptibly differently to relieve stress on a certain area. But you can't relieve stress in one place without transferring it to another. As such, we wanted to nip this thing in the bud.

Luckily, Steph is a pro's pro. She got on it right away and her doctor prescribed antibiotics that ended up clearing things up quite quickly. By

---

[2] UTMB stands for Ultra-Trail du Mont-Blanc—the most prestigious ultra trail race in the world. HOKA is the title sponsor of the event and makes a huge deal of the entire week which consists of several ultra trail races, not just UTMB—many either starting or finishing in beautiful Chamonix, a commune in the southeastern region of France.

Saturday, the foot didn't affect the long run at all. She ran twenty miles total with miles 15-19 in 5:35, 5:35, 5:30 and 5:39. It was a beautifully executed run and she felt good about it afterwards, knowing that a marathon training build takes patience. In fact, patience has been a virtue for Steph in her career since joining NAZ Elite in 2014.

When I joined the team, my initial thoughts were like, alright, let's get ready to make this Olympic Team, and then it did switch for me since I got pregnant again [in 2015]. Then I was like, wow, what does my career look like? What does this mean? Am I done because now I had a second baby? I hadn't heard of too many women having two babies that close together [and running at a high level], or they weren't talking about it. I think I was a little nervous because I was like, 'Are you going to be invested? Do you think I'm serious because I got pregnant again? Is HOKA invested?' There were all these kinds of questions so I was apprehensive and I [said to myself], 'Hey you need to prove that you can come back from these children, you can do all the things that are possible.'

I was lucky that I was fully financially supported by you guys, and everyone was on board to let me go at my own pace, and my own timeline, and when I look back that was seven, eight years ago, I mean, everything worked out perfectly. I can't imagine any other path to get to now.

As I myself look back at that time period, first of all it seems like a long time ago which I guess it was. But the entire NAZ Elite phase of my life is one of those things that sometimes feels like it started yesterday, and sometimes feels like I've been doing this forever. Things kind of run together so I have to really sit down and think about it to get the timelines right. Steph was the same way when I asked her about how she remembers the beginning. What we both remember clearly, though, was how diligent we were in coming back to running after Steph had Riley in June of 2014. That was such a calculated decision on Steph's part—as are so many of the decisions she makes when it comes to her career. She wanted to start a family, but she wanted to do it in such a way so as to allow her to be safely back at her best come the 2016 Olympic Trials Marathon.

Once she started running again in the fall of 2014, after her first pregnancy, we would meet every Sunday at a coffee shop in town and have a chat about the previous week and talk about what she'd be able to handle in the week to come. Our priority was staying healthy and slowly building back into full training, always letting the body drive the ship. It was actually a really enjoyable period because it was almost like coaching a high school freshman where you're seeing real tangible progress each and every week. And then, all of a sudden, things regressed.

We're training, and you're giving me workouts, and then all of a sudden, I was like, 'Man, I thought my postpartum would be a little smoother.' And it was interesting for you, I think, because we were meeting weekly and you were listening to my feedback and learning. And I thought we built back so well, and then I did this time trial up here in early 2015, on the track, and it went...so bad. And it was like, 'Oh my gosh, am I low on iron? And you were like, 'I don't really know. Is this just postpartum?' And then I found out I was pregnant with Hudson.

For me as a coach, I think the best thing I did during that entire stretch from 2014 when Steph joined the team, until the fall of 2015—after she had her second child, was to be realistic with expectations about 2016. When an athlete has their mind set on something, like Steph did for the 2016 Olympic Trials Marathon—probably from the moment she stepped off the course at the 2012 Trials, it is very hard to get them to step back and see the bigger picture. I had to do that with Steph. If I would have allowed her to convince me that we should be aggressive and try to run the 2016 Trials, just five months postpartum, it could have ruined her career. It really could have. And I just believed in my heart of hearts that there was so much more for her to accomplish.

I think the way I put it to her was this, "Look, if you find yourself daydreaming about being ready for the Trials on an easy run this fall, I'm not saying that's a bad thing. Maybe it's good because it will keep you motivated as you come back. But I have to be honest and tell you that it's most likely not going to happen."

It's so tempting as a coach to tell an athlete what they want to hear, but it's so much better to tell them the truth. And then a very cool thing happens. Because when you tell them the truth, as long as they're willing to accept it, and what you said turns out to be right, they will have a faith in you that runs way deeper than it would have otherwise—there will be true trust.

I think Steph has had true trust in me ever since. And that made my job so much easier. I've continued to be honest with her, I've continued to be realistic with my expectations, and as a result if we go into a race and I tell her I think she can run a certain time, or finish in a certain place, or win…she believes it.

STEPH'S TRAINING THIS WEEK:

Monday: Rest Day

Tuesday: 14 mile easy run

Wednesday: AM – 8 mile easy run
PM – 4 mile easy run

Thursday: AM – Fartlek. 1 minute, 2 minutes, 3 minutes, 2 minutes, 1 minute, 2 minutes, 3 minutes, 2 minutes, 1 minute, 2 minutes, 3minutes (with equal rest after each). 11 miles total.
PM – 4 mile easy run

Friday: AM – 9 mile easy run
PM – 4 mile easy run

Saturday: 20 mile long run with the last 4 miles at marathon effort.

Sunday: 8 mile easy run

Total Weekly Mileage: 78 miles

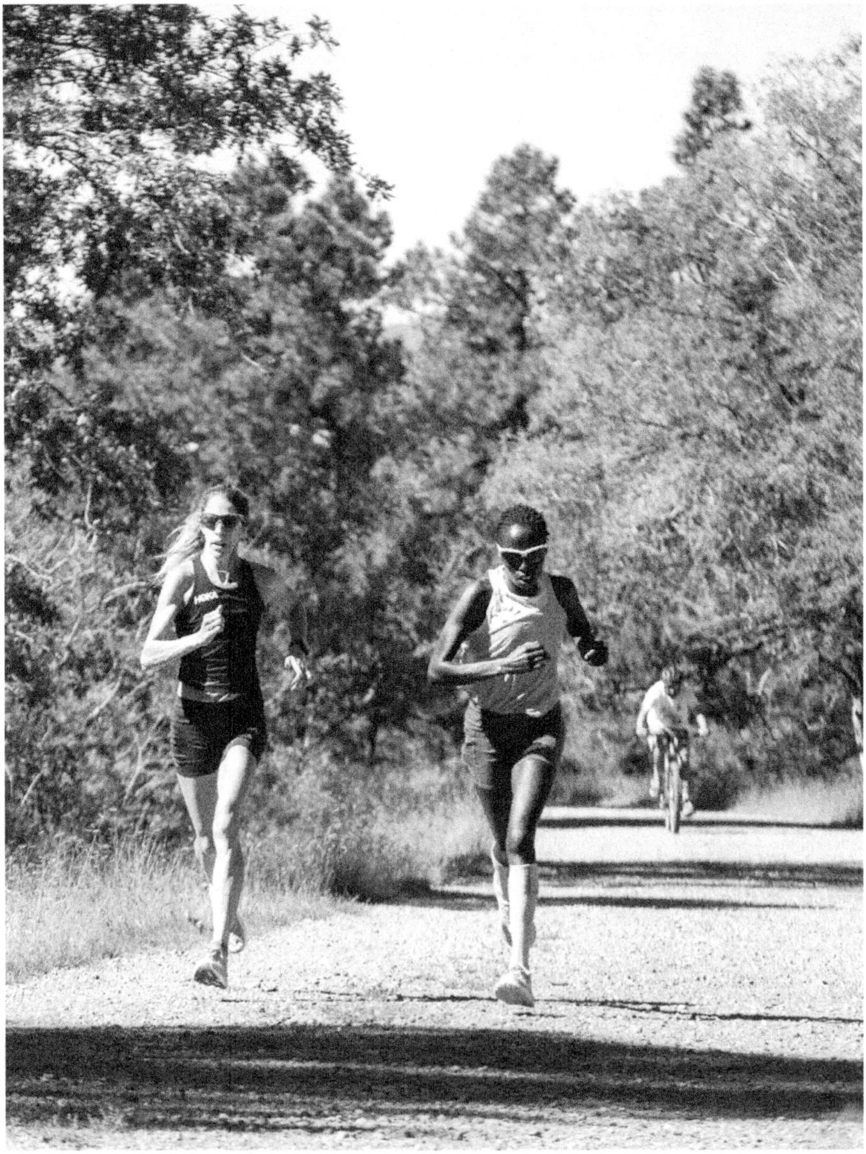

CHAPTER 3.0

Sisters

10 WEEKS OUT FROM THE NYC MARATHON
AUGUST 29TH – SEPTEMBER 4TH

After finishing up what was a fairly easy stretch post NACAC Champs, it was back to business this week for Steph with two hard sessions on the docket and a total of nearly 100 miles. The first workout was going to be another chance for Steph to overlap with Aliphine, and at Buffalo Park no less.[1] Aliphine pretty much owns Buffalo. Really, they should give her a deed to the land. But the cool thing about Steph when it comes to working out with Allie is that she loves it. She knows it makes her better.

We are both not afraid to be like, 'I want to kick your butt,' in workouts because we know that that is what is going to get us to the next level. What I learned from her specifically in 2018, in some of the workouts where I was kind of like, 'Okay I should be more calculated,' she was kind of like, 'I don't give a shit,' so I was like, 'Maybe I should do that sometimes,' and that I think helped me go into races thinking differently. I was like, 'Are these people that much better than me or are they just taking risks and maybe I'm not?' Ultimately that led to me winning Peachtree, my first national championship, and I do attribute a lot of that to Aliphine, and learning from her, and absorbing her attitude.

Tuesday's session, specifically, was as follows:

2-mile tempo run at marathon effort
3 minutes rest
2-mile hill circuit (the circuit includes a 150-meter stride at 3k effort, a 250-meter uphill at 5k effort, a 600 meter gentle downhill at marathon effort, a flat 200-meter stride at mile effort, and finally a 600-meter uphill at half marathon effort)
3 minutes rest
2-mile tempo run at half marathon effort

---

[1] Buffalo Park is a city park in Flagstaff with a hilly 2-mile dirt/gravel loop, marked every quarter mile. The loop's final 300 meters includes a nasty uphill that makes even the fittest athletes in the world gasp for air.

3 minutes rest

2-mile hill circuit

I rode along on my bike, partially to keep a close eye on things, partially to get some exercise, and partially because it wasn't lost on me that I wouldn't get to see these two working out together too many more times. I was glad I did too because, like so many times before, they nailed it. It was a thing of beauty to watch them work together on the first 2-mile, running it just a hair faster than the prescribed 11:20 (you saw what Steph had to say about Aliphine's workouts). Aliphine ran about 11:11 with Steph two ticks back in 11:13. Then they were stride for stride on the entire hill circuit. Interestingly, one would probably think Aliphine is better on hills than Steph—just because of the way she looks like she's attacking with every step she takes. I would say though, and so would Allie, that Steph is actually the one that leads the way on the ups. However, Allie is better on the downs so it evens out over the course of the circuit.

On the second two-mile tempo I wanted things to be a bit more free. Alan and I had talked about a wait-and-see approach to determine a goal time based on how the workout was going to that point. I knew Aliphine would want to push that second tempo a bit with the USATF 20k Championships coming up next week. She likes to feel that hurt just a bit so she can have the confidence she needs on race day. That's just how she operates, and she'd definitely need to be confident because she was going to be up against the American record holder in the marathon, Keira D'Amato, and American half marathon record holder, Emily Sisson.

Steph, though, just needed a solid tempo right at her half marathon effort, nothing more. So that's pretty much what I told them before the repeat. I said, "Let's shoot for true half marathon effort, or let's call it 20k effort for Aliphine's sake, on this one. There might be a little separation and that's okay. Just focus on yourselves."

When you've worked with athletes as long as I've worked with Steph and Allie, there are certain phrases that have sort of hidden meanings. This was basically me saying, "Aliphine can get moving on this one a bit, but Steph—don't get sucked in."

And she didn't. Aliphine ran 10:55 and Steph ran 11:05, which were both totally appropriate. It is such a pleasure working with veteran athletes who know themselves so well. On the last hill circuit I gave no instructions, hidden or otherwise, and was certainly hoping to see them stay together just as they had the first time through. And outside of Allie pulling away a little bit on the long downhill, which was to be expected, they were side by side once again.

Sports is a funny thing in the sense that when an athlete is your opponent, and you don't know much about them, they are essentially your enemy. But almost always, when you get to know them, and especially if they join your team, they become your friend. Or from a fan's perspective there's that player you hate on the other team, and you boo them, and you have nothing good to think of them, and then they sign with your team and boom; you buy their jersey.

When Aliphine got her American citizenship in 2016, I am not speaking for Steph here, but I certainly remember thinking to myself, "Oh no. She's a threat to Kellyn making the Olympic team in the 10,000." That's all I cared about. Kellyn was on our team. My vested interest was in Kellyn. Everyone else was our opponent and I wanted to beat them.[2] Pretty simple.

I asked Steph how she remembers getting to know Aliphine.

When Aliphine came onto the scene I was like, 'Who is this woman? She's dominating all these races.' I had never met her. At the 10 Mile Champs in 2016 she came up to me and said, 'Oh my gosh you're the lady with those two babies.' So she had kind of followed me, and I could just tell that she was like, 'What is this all about, how are you doing this?' She was so far away from thinking about having children.

And that 10 Mile Champs went terrible for me, but again it was like, 'I'm out here, putting in the work.' I think I was 11th or 12th.

And then I kind of kept seeing Aliphine at road races and then we were on the World Cross Country Team together in Uganda in 2017. And that race was great because [the U.S. team] didn't know each other very well, and she didn't really know how good our team was. And I was like, 'I think if we all perform we could have a great day.' And she goes out and finishes 15th, even though she lost her shoe, and then she goes right into the tent probably thinking, 'I don't know where everyone else is.' And then I finish 22nd, and Natosha Rogers

---

[2] Aliphine was indeed a threat, but at the 2016 Olympic Trials Kellyn finished fourth and Aliphine finished seventh. Just sayin'!

finishes right behind me, and then Sarah Pagano, and I was like, 'Oh my gosh, we did awesome.' And so I walked into the tent and Aliphine's like, ya know, doing whatever, and I'm like, 'Aliphine, I think we got fifth,' and she just jumps up and screams 'Oh my gosh…way to go ladies.'

I loved hearing that story because even though I wasn't there I can see Aliphine jumping up and down. I can hear her screaming. Her energy is so contagious and has become such a vital part of our overall team mojo. We are better because she joined us, period. And it goes way beyond her performances. She and Steph and Kellyn, in particular, have something that goes way beyond sports.

I think the bond that Aliphine and I have, it started as teammates, but then it grew as friends, and then women who share so many common life goals, like wanting to have families. I was a mom, her wanting to be a mom. The balance of it all. But also being really fierce competitors. And then wanting to bring out the best in each other. It's all gone uphill and we've become very close, and yeah, she's like a sister to me. We call each other sister. I don't know, it's a different kind of relationship than you'd ever have with a co-worker. It feels so much more special when you're invested in one another's successes and failures. It's on and off the race course, and it just runs really deep.

Unfortunately, the very next day after the workout at Buffalo Park, Aliphine noticed some swelling in her ankle, but she hadn't twisted it. She saw her physio, A.J. Gregg, on Thursday and he was concerned immediately. I texted him that evening and he sent me a one sentence reply.

I would be very careful with this

Message received. I spoke to him the following morning and he made it very clear that the injury could very well be in the medial malleolus, the bony bump on the inside of the ankle, a bone that you do not want to mess with. Apparently, that particular bone takes a long time to heal and if you let it get too bad, can require surgery. None of this sounded good at all. I spoke to Aliphine that day and of course, she was devastated. We had to pull out of the 20k Championships, one of her favorite races, and for at least the weekend we were going to have to avoid putting any pressure on the bone—which meant no running. The plan is to get an MRI next week. After that, we'll know much more.

When you hear news like that for one athlete, it's so tough to avoid letting that bleed over into your mood when you see the others. But you have to separate your negative feelings and bring the positivity to the next session. For Steph, she had a big cutdown long run on Sunday and so I showed up ready to coach, ready to give her the encouragement she needed, and I put my sadness for Allie on the backburner. And of course Steph had to do the same. She knew Aliphine had pulled out of the 20k, which of course meant something serious was going on, but she stayed focused on the task at hand: a 20-mile run with the last 10 miles cutting down from 6:30 per mile all the way down to 5:20 (if possible).

She pretty much nailed it. With temps getting into the 80s by the end of the run, it was tough to ratchet the pace all the way down to 5:20. But she sure tried. Splits for her last 10 miles:

6:23, 6:22, 6:16, 6:14, 6:08, 5:59, 5:48, 5:38, 5:32, 5:35 for an average of 6:00 per mile overall. With the 10 easy miles beforehand, and a 2-mile cool-down, Steph knocked out 22 miles on the day. Mission accomplished.

On to the next…

STEPH'S TRAINING THIS WEEK:

Monday: AM – 9 mile easy run
PM – 4 mile easy run

Tuesday: hill circuits at Buffalo Park. 2-mile tempo. 3 minutes rest. 2-mile hill circuit. 3 minutes rest. 2-mile tempo. 3 minutes rest. 2-mile hill circuit. 14 miles total.

Wednesday: AM – 10 mile easy run
PM – 4 mile easy run

Thursday: AM – 8 mile easy run
PM – 4 mile easy run

Friday: AM – 14 mile "easy" run (up to Mt Elden and back)
PM – 4 mile easy run

Saturday: 8 mile easy run

Sunday: 10 miles easy, 10 mile cutdown, 2-mile cool-down for 22 on the day.

Total Weekly Mileage: 98 miles

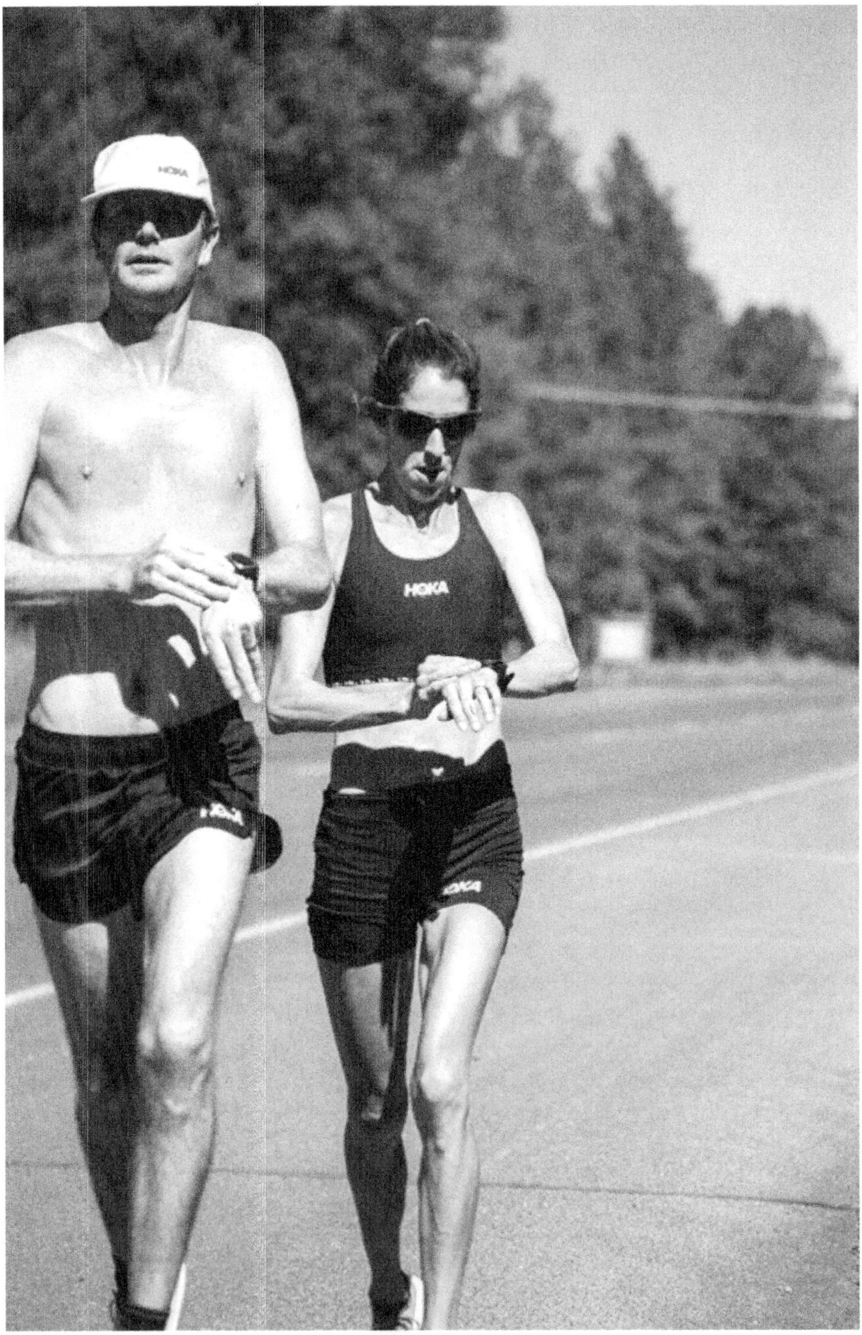

CHAPTER 4.0

Happy Birthday Ben B

9 WEEKS OUT FROM THE NYC MARATHON
SEPTEMBER 5TH – 11TH

From January of 2014 through the spring of 2022, I spent every Sunday afternoon thinking about each and every athlete on our team, what they needed the coming week, and then putting their training into Final Surge—the online platform we use for coach/athlete communication.[1] Only last month, after Alice Wright ran the European Marathon

---

[1] finalsurge.com - check it out!

Championships on August 15, was I finally at a point where Alan and Jenna had taken on this task to the extent that I could (mostly) relax on a Sunday. Because Alice had already started her training segment for Euros when Alan came on board, I continued to lead the way throughout that entire block. I also continued writing Aliphine's training through the spring, which was pretty satisfying seeing as she went on a run that included a runner-up finish at the Pittsburgh Half Marathon, a win at the USATF 25k Championships, a win at the BOLDERBoulder 10k, and a massive run at the Mastercard Mini 10k where she was fourth against a world class field in 31:08—a personal best by a full minute. And finally, there was Steph. For her, we had decided on a collaboration. I really liked Alan's theory that what Steph needed was for her workouts to be very controlled—lots of work in the right zones but with very few "monster" sessions. It made sense to me because Steph never likes to get overly competitive in workouts. She always tries to hit the splits spot on, not "beat" them like so many other athletes. Instead, she saves the competition for race day. For my money, she can get more out of herself in a race than just about anyone I have ever worked with.

What really set things in motion as far as how this entire segment would work was a meeting on August 5 between myself, Alan, Jenna, and Steph. We met in a tiny breakout room at NACET—a non-profit office and manufacturing space for local companies in the tech, engineering, and sustainable energy sectors.[2] Alan and I had prepped for the meeting by outlining Steph's schedule all the way through New York. I had written the original draft based on what I believed to be Steph's best marathon segment ever—the buildup to the 2020 Olympic Trials. But I had highlighted spots where I felt Alan could change things and institute some double workout days that would consist of a very controlled workout in the morning and another very controlled workout in the afternoon (more on these later). Then I had kept some of our biggest marathon specific long runs in stone, if you will, believing that we needed these to be properly prepared for the demands of the marathon—specifically the NYC Marathon—which I believe requires more strength than most.

The next hour in that room was everything I believe this team can be moving forward. We were treating an athlete as an individual—respecting that everyone is unique and has their own physical and mental strengths and weaknesses. We were giving that athlete an opportunity to share her thoughts and opinions about those strengths and weaknesses. And our entire staff was present and participating in the process. One thing I always tried to avoid during my years as head coach was for this to be "Ben's team." I think that's a poor business model but you see that with other professional running groups in the U.S. I much prefer the stick and ball sports model where the team, the entity, is bigger than any one

---

[2] NACET stands for Northern Arizona Center for Entrepreneurship and Technology. In addition to the tech, engineering, and sustainable energy companies housed in the building are some more general organizations that bring jobs to Flagstaff including Hypo2 Chiropractic owned by brothers A.J. and Wes Gregg. A.J. and Wes are our team's chiropractors as well as our strength and conditioning coaches. We've worked with them since our team launched in 2014.

individual—star athletes and big-time coaches included. When that's the case, a team can afford to lose a big star, or decide to make a coaching change, and the ethos of the team remains intact. And most importantly, the fans stick with the team. Because, in my opinion—and I think it's more fact than opinion, the value of a team lies with its fans.

Steph understands all of this better than most athletes out there. As an entrepreneur herself, she understood that Picky Bars had to be about more than Steph, Lauren, and Jesse. And it was. I would venture to say that's part of why this transition never seemed to scare her. Plus, she knows I have her best interest at heart, always. If I didn't think Alan, and his input, could help her in this, her final season, we wouldn't have had that meeting, period. So inherently, the meeting was important because she knows I wouldn't waste her time. Thus, Alan's comments that day held real weight, and I could tell Steph really liked what he had to say. I walked away believing that we had something special. One of my first conversations with Alan afterward was that I thought he should start writing Steph's training after the NACAC Champs with me as a consultant each week.

So that's what we did. The first week of Alan being "in charge" of Steph's schedule was the easy-ish week coming off of NACAC. Then last week was the first bigger week and it was smooth sailing. When I checked out this week, I did have a little worry that he had pulled back on the mileage too much. Even though she's two weeks out from the USATF road 10k Champs on September 17, I knew from her past that she didn't need to back off this far out from a race that was merely a step toward NYC. I knew NYC mattered more.

Text exchange between me and Alan on Sunday, September 5, 2022:

Me: Do we want Steph at around 100 miles again this week? FS has quite a bit less listed right now.

Alan: Was going to ask what you thought based on previous experience and her being able to race off higher mileage.

Me: For sure closer to 100 this week. Could probably go 6/6 on Thursday after the double workout on Wednesday, 10/4 on Friday, and 6/4 on Sunday. That'd be 96 total.

Alan: That all sounds good! Thanks for verifying

So Steph—when you read this I'm sorry. Alan had you at about 75 miles. The 98 you had to do was my fault.

The week went really well though, at least physically. On Wednesday, Steph had a double workout day, with a workout in the morning and another in the afternoon. I facilitated her morning session, riding along on the bike as she knocked out a 6-mile progression run on Lake Mary Road. It was nothing fancy; her mile splits were 6:40, 6:28, 6:12, 5:58, 5:45, 5:22. With a one-mile warmup and a one-mile cool-down she knocked out 8 miles for the morning and got right back home to recover with the harder of the day's sessions scheduled for the afternoon.

That p.m. workout was meant to be run on a track but Steph had to drop Hudson off at his soccer tryouts at a field that really wasn't close to any of the tracks in town so she asked if she could do it on a road near the fields.[3] That way she could drop him off, do the workout while he was at soccer, and pick him up after—never missing a beat. We said, "No problem," and Alan got out there early with the measuring wheel and marked off a course for her. I have always appreciated the pragmatic approach Steph takes to things like that. Some athletes would freak out, and prioritize finding a track, placing importance on the wrong thing. Steph understands physiology. The point of the workout was the work itself, not the surface.

And the work for this one was 16 x 400 meters with a scant 45 seconds recovery. The plan called for each 400 to be run in 77-78 seconds, and in typical Steph fashion, she nailed it. Officially her splits were: 78, 76, 79, 76, 78, 75, 77, 74, 77, 74, 77, 74, 77, 74, 76, 74. As you can perhaps tell, the road wasn't completely flat, hence the difference in times between the slightly uphill repeats and the slightly downhill ones, but again—she understood what Alan wanted and kept the effort the same throughout. With the USATF 10k Championships coming up in a week-and-a-half on a hilly course, and the New York Marathon being hilly as well, a little up and down was probably better than the track anyway. Like so many things thus far in this segment, it all worked out.

While Wednesday was great, Thursday was one of those days as a coach that challenges your ability to compartmentalize. Aliphine's MRI came

---

[3] He made the team.

back and the results were not good. Not terrible, but not good. There was a small amount of marrow edema in the anterior aspect of the medial malleolus. In addition, there was evidence of a near complete tear of the anterior talofibular ligament, and of a thickening of the Achilles tendon, consistent with tendinosis. At this point, it seems like New York City is out. I'm gutted for her. Nine days ago, after her workout at Buffalo Park, I would have told you that Aliphine was going to win the USATF 20k Championships on Labor Day and that New York was going to be a very special day. Now we may be looking at six to eight weeks off.

But life goes on and that evening was Ben Bruce's 40th birthday party. Steph had worked really hard putting the whole thing together, and I couldn't go there in a shitty mood just because my mind was on Aliphine's diagnosis. Jen and I and Addison got ready and headed over to the Bruce's, excited to celebrate Ben's big day. Steph had hired a professional chef to cater the affair, and invited just a few close friends. She had suggested on the invite that you dress up, which I took to mean a collared shirt and nice jeans. I mean, for Flagstaff, a collared shirt and nice jeans is pretty darn dressy. Whoops. We walked in and Ben was in a sweet wedding-reception-quality suit, then Kyle Taylor and Eric Fernandez arrived in suits as well.[4] Gosh darn it. Anyway, there was some before-dinner champagne so I quickly forgot about my lack of style. The night was really fun and it was cool to celebrate Ben. Steph has sort of been the public star of the

---

[4] Eric is not only a former teammate of Ben and Steph's, part of the original NAZ roster, but he is now their financial advisor. Seeing our athletes succeed after their running career is over is something I really enjoy.

Bruce's for a long time now, but as she said in her toast that night, "Ben takes care of this whole family."

I asked Steph to expand a little bit on that for the book:

He is the organizer, but he's the organizer in ways that I'm not organized. And then I'm organized in ways that he's not organized. I'm always booking appointments, I'm always doing this and that. We butt heads sometimes about what's more important. So he almost takes on what you would think is the traditional 'mom role,' right, all the things he does. He makes sure the boys are always taken care of. He cooks for the whole family. He does our laundry. I wouldn't say he cleans the house, but certain parts of the house. He's in charge of the kitchen, dishes, the yard...and then we balance the rest.

He also kind of plans his days around my training. And then obviously he's our official pacer for the group. But he's always aware of making sure he isn't just pacing workouts that I'm in, he wants to make sure he's pacing all the other women too.

I also asked her to talk about the initial attraction between she and Ben:

I would say initially I was like, 'I don't know. This guy is kind of interesting,' because I went to his house in San Luis Obispo, I drove up from Santa Barbara. I went to the wrong house, and he watched me from his window go to the wrong house. He did not come out and say, 'You're at the wrong house.' So first of all,

I'm thinking he's an a-hole.[5] He basically watched the neighbor point across the street. So I walked over there. It was pretty awkward because we didn't really know each other, and he was like, 'Are you hungry?' [Starts laughing] So I'm thinking, 'Yeah, he's gonna suggest we go somewhere.' And he goes, 'Do you want a tuna sandwich?' I said, 'I guess.' [Laughing harder now] So he just went in the kitchen and made me a fucking tuna melt.[6]

But it was so perfect because that's so Ben. He didn't want to do all these bells and whistles. Men are always like, 'Let me take you out to this expensive place.' But that's not who he is. He was just like, 'This is me. I have plenty of food to cook in the kitchen. You're hungry. I'm going to make you a tuna melt.'

Saturday morning was a welcome change, weather-wise. I woke up to rain and it made me happy. Now that might not sound cheery at first, but after a pretty hot couple of weeks (by Flagstaff standards), and knowing that Steph was going to have to bang out a hard 20 miles, the rain meant cooler temps and, mostly likely, a good workout. It was also Ben's actual birthday and I was looking forward to razzing him about turning 40 in person. All those things considered, I was probably a little more excited than normal to get to practice and so I was the first one to arrive.

I pulled into the little parking alcove nestled in the forest along Lake Mary Rd., our meeting spot for the day, a couple of minutes before 8:30 a.m. To my surprise, the next car to pull in belonged to Kellyn. I say surprise

---

[5] She really said "a-hole." Steph rarely curses.

[6] I said rarely.

because a) Kellyn is notoriously late and b) I didn't even know she'd be joining. Since she told us she was pregnant, the coaching staff decided unanimously that it made the most sense for Alan to take on her training so as to allow the two of them to build a relationship before she comes back to full training sometime next year. By that time, the NAZ coaching transition will be complete and Alan will have the reins in full. We'll also be less than a year out from the 2024 Olympic Trials Marathon at that point and Kellyn will need to put her complete faith in Alan to get her where she wants to go. Better to get that entire process going now. As such, I am not privy to the conversations they're having about what she'll be doing each week. Nor should I be. But it was great to see her and I was happy she'd be jumping in.

When Ben and Steph arrived, they got out of the car clearly still in the middle of some sort of semi-serious conversation, so I hung with Kellyn for a second while they finished up. Then I got my first chance to razz Ben. He was wearing a black HOKA jacket with a bunch of red, orange, and yellow color pops along all sorts of pockets and zippers.

I said, "Dang…look at that 40-year-old in his fancy jacket."

Turns out he had gotten it at UTMB, it was the same jacket some of the Ultra runners had to have for the race—multiple pockets and zippers being required for ventilation, food storage, sunscreen, anti-chafe cream, and gosh knows what else. 100-plus miles is a long way for crying out loud.

Anyway, you could tell Ben was in a good mood. He pretty much always is. Same goes for Steph.[7]

But even though she had a smile on her face, she was tired. She joked about how she didn't want to do yesterday's second run and about how this morning she fantasized what it would be like if she just said, "You know what…I'm just not going to do this today."

Some fantasy huh? That's a marathoner for ya.

Anyway, a couple of minutes later Ben, Steph, and Kellyn were off on their warmup and I hopped back in my car and drove to the Circle K to get a donut. Truthfully, I just had to go to the bathroom, but I have this thing where I feel guilty if I use a gas station bathroom and don't buy anything. So yes, I really did get a donut—chocolate with chocolate frosting. It was delicious.

That was that, and twenty minutes later we were ready to roll.

Lake Mary Road, where Steph has run at least a couple hundred workouts over the last decade, is an idyllic place for marathoners. Overall, it's a 53-mile stretch of road with wide shoulders that runs mostly north-south from Flagstaff to Arizona State Route 87—a road that then takes you to the

---

[7] Gosh it's going to be tough when they're not around anymore. I hope that's a long time from now as I hope Ben will stick around as the team's pacer and I hope Steph will stick around in pretty much any capacity she wants.

small towns of Strawberry and Payson. Depending on the workout, we use some or all of a 16-mile section that starts about two miles from the road's northernmost point in Flagstaff. For today's session we were set to run from our "start" to the 10-mile mark and back. The workout called for Steph to alternate miles at 6:40 and 5:40 for all 20. This has been a classic for us over the years. Before the Trials we did this session down in Camp Verde, Ariz. at 3100 feet above sea level so the paces were faster (6:30 and 5:30). We have to adjust things in Flagstaff for the extra altitude though. Lake Mary sits at about 6800 feet, thus 6:40 and 5:40.[8]

Right before the three of them took off I made a joke about the day—something to the effect of, "A 40-year-old, a pregnant lady, and Steph…here we go."

As a coach, it's always good to be appropriately light before a workout begins, I think. The easier the session, the lighter you can be. The harder the session, you may want to be a little more locked in but you still have to be calm and confident. The athletes will be plenty nervous and you don't want to make it any worse. I'd say today, as crazy as it may sound, wasn't really meant to be that hard. It's more of a prerequisite for what's to come

---

[8] There are a number of online calculators that will spit out altitude conversions for you. However, it's been my experience that some athletes have a little less of a conversion than others. Specifically, athletes who were born and raised at altitude, like Aliphine, seem to be able to run closer to sea level paces when training at altitude than athletes like Steph, who were not. But then there are athletes like Kellyn who, over time, seem to be able to chip away at their conversion. I think Steph has done that as well, but not to the extent that Kellyn has. The bottom line is that there is definitely a conversion, but you have to allow for some individual variance when calculating it.

in a few weeks when we'll be running 5:40s for 15-16 miles straight. No jokes right before that one.

Plus, today we had Ben. The birthday boy is the best pacer out there. He knows Lake Mary better than anyone in the world. I don't think that's hyperbole. He knows the ups and downs of each mile, he knows how much a headwind will slow you down, how much a tailwind will help, and he takes all these things into consideration when he's pacing a session. I really don't have to worry about the athletes being too fast, or too slow, if he's out there.

He also knows the spirit of each workout, meaning he knows what we're trying to accomplish. Basically, he thinks like a coach, and serves that role when he's out there—feeding the athletes little bits of wisdom and encouragement along the way. And today he knew that the 6:40s are hard to hit spot on. Often, we'll be a little fast on those because for the first few seconds of the "off" mile you're still decelerating from the previous pace and the last few seconds you're often naturally speeding up a bit to get some momentum going into the next "on." Still, the fastest he was today on any of the 6:40s was a 6:29, and that was on a mile with a net downhill. The guy's amazing.

Steph was equally amazing, as was Kellyn who, at five months pregnant, made it 8 miles. Crazy. I don't mind putting into writing the fact that if Kellyn were to make the Olympic marathon team in 2024 it would be the greatest moment in the history of our team, bar none. And I believe it's possible. Steph tweeted this after the workout, along with a video of the two of them running:

She would never put this out herself but this morning @kellyntaylor ran 8 miles alternating 5:40/6:30 at 7000ft, 5 months pregnant. So yeah, she's gonna kick everyone's butt when she comes back after having a baby next year and years to come!

I agree.

After Kellyn finished, it was down to Steph and Ben for the next several miles until Ben was also out of gas—stepping off with six miles to go.[9] The final four miles of this one were uphill, by design, to mimic the closing miles in New York City where the runners have to climb up Fifth Avenue from the Bronx toward Central Park, and then deal with a number of ups and downs over the last five kilometers to the finish. Today, each of Steph's final four miles finished higher than it started and in total she gained 140 feet during that stretch. And yet, her last four miles were still perfectly executed; she ran them in 6:37, 5:34, 6:37, 5:33. Overall, she ran 20 miles in 2:01:45 (a 6:05 per mile average). Eight weeks and one day out from NYC, we're right where we want to be.

---

[9] To be fair to Ben, he had also paced another NAZ workout the day before.

STEPH'S TRAINING THIS WEEK:

Monday: 10 mile easy run

Tuesday: AM – 8.5 mile easy run
PM – 3.5 mile easy run

Wednesday: AM – 6 mile progression run
PM – 16 x 400 with 45 seconds rest

Thursday: AM – 5 mile easy run
PM – 7 mile easy run

Friday: AM – 10 mile easy run
PM – 4 mile easy run

Saturday: 20 mile alternating pace long run

Sunday: AM – 6 mile easy run
PM – 4 mile easy run

Total Weekly Mileage: 98 miles

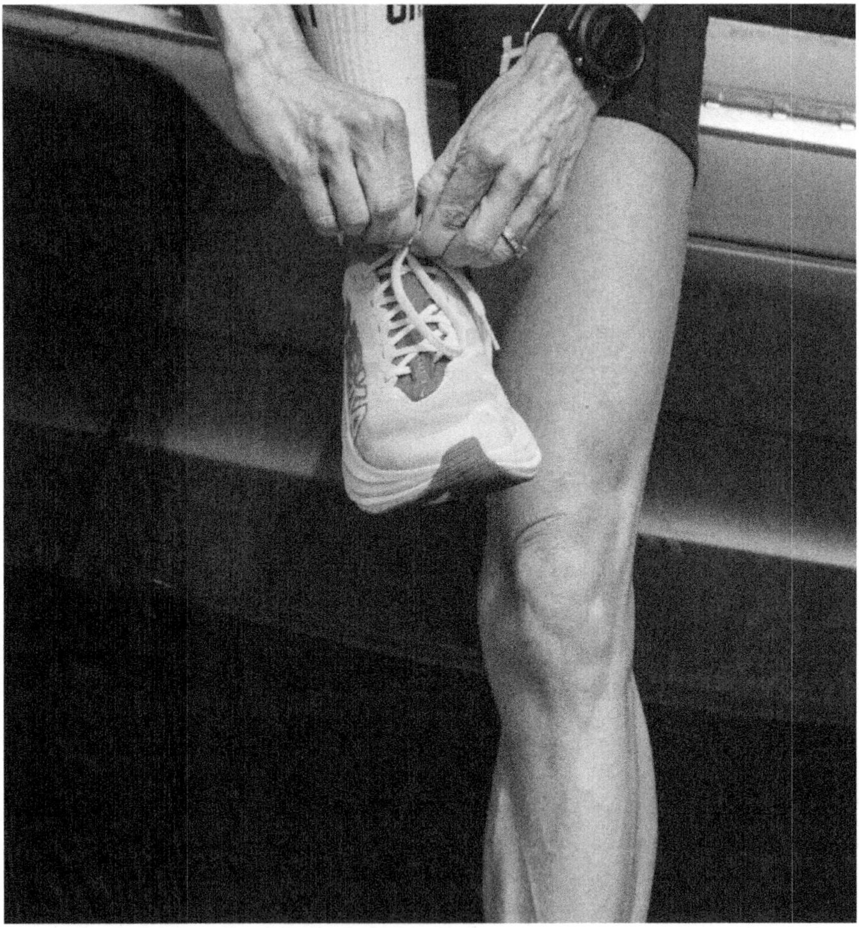

CHAPTER 4.5

The Ingebrigtsen Factor

This entire chapter was unplanned, and is the result of something that happened to me as I wrote the previous chapter. So here goes:

I was so pumped after the Saturday morning session, and happy with how Steph's segment is going, that I wanted to make sure I wrote my thoughts down right away. I came home, got some lunch, and got down to it. First though, I went back to check on a quote that I included in chapter 0.0—the one from Steph about losing her dad when she was a senior in high school. I had included what I remembered her saying as sort of a placeholder but needed to go back and get it exactly right. To do so, I had to watch *A Time And A Place*—the documentary about our team as we prepared for, and eventually competed at, the 2020 Olympic Trials Marathon. I had planned on simply fast forwarding to the part where Steph speaks about her dad, but I got sucked in. I don't think I had watched the movie in full since HOKA showed it at the Olympic Track Trials in the summer of 2021. Wow. It was powerful, and I wasn't prepared for that. When you're in it, something as intense as trying to make an Olympic Team, you're just in it. You don't have time to reflect. And then you move on to the next thing, and for me that next thing was keeping up the team's morale during the pandemic, and then it was hiring a new coach, and expanding the entire vision for what NAZ is…and is going to be. It was a whirlwind.

But watching the documentary turned out to be quite cathartic. I am not sure I had ever really come to terms with exactly why I wanted to move on from the head coaching role, to focus on the director role instead. The reason I shared publicly, which was true, was that I like new challenges and I saw the expansion of the team as exactly that. However, after watching that Trials segment unfold on the screen, and feeling (all over again) the emotion of those few months—the ecstasy of Aliphine's victory and the agony for Steph and Kellyn, and for Scott Fauble and Scott Smith and Sid Vaughn, I think simply calling all of this a new challenge was certainly the simple version. The more complicated, and ultimately truer, version is that deep down I wondered if I could ever be as invested in coaching a group of athletes as I was coaching those six, during those three months, again. Ever. And believe me I tried. I poured everything I had into the summer of 2020—into keeping us fired up when Covid had shut everything down.

And then I rallied again that fall, preparing seven athletes for the Marathon Project—an event I co-directed.[1] And those segments went well, they really did. I don't think anyone, myself included, ever noticed a difference.

But in 2021 I noticed. That was the first time that things weren't as fun. Perhaps it's a chicken and the egg situation, but at the end of the year a couple of our athletes left the team.[2] Did they leave because I wasn't the coach I once was, because they no longer believed in me, because I was forcing things? Or was I forcing things because I didn't believe in them? Because they weren't giving us, and me, the same level of buy-in as that

---

[1] The world pretty much shut down in March of 2020. The running world was no different. All races and meets were canceled, including the Olympic Track and Field Trials and the Olympic Games. All marathons in the United States were canceled for the remainder of the year. So in August, my former business partner, Matt Helbig, and my good friend Josh Cox, and I, partnered on a plan to host a professionals-only marathon in December in Arizona that could serve as a chance for North American-based marathoners to compete. It was basically a full-time job for the next three-plus months but we pulled it off. We held it at a resort in Chandler, Ariz. called Wild Horse Pass. The course was as flat and fast as you could possibly imagine and the weather was ideal. The athletes were amazing and ended up producing a heck of a show. Martin Hehir won the men's race in 2:08:59 and Sara Hall won the women's race in 2:20:32. All told, seven men broke 2:10 and 12 women broke 2:30. It was a historic day and something I am very proud to have been a part of.

[2] Four athletes in total left the team at the end of 2021. Scott Smith, with his wife expecting their first child, retired after an awesome career. I couldn't have been happier for him. Sid Vaughn, unfortunately, wasn't able to stay healthy during his time at NAZ and we parted ways mutually. I hope against hope he'll be able to figure things out moving forward. Scott Fauble and Rory Linkletter left because they wanted a change. Pissed off as I may have been at the time, I now harbor no ill will toward either of them. I didn't take it personally, but I did take it as a huge challenge from the business side and their leaving drives me still to this day.

group in 2020? It's all very nuanced. And hiding out beneath the entire thing, a giant elephant in the room at the time, was what the athletes were wearing, or in this case not wearing, on their feet.

"Super Shoes," so named because of the almost astronomical effect they had on performance, had come onto the scene as early as 2016–though only Nike had made them and basically kept it a secret.[3] By the end of 2021, pretty much all the other major brands had their own version of a

---

[3] Super shoes really began being worn in 2016 at the U.S. Olympic Trials Marathon but no one, save for a select few, knew it. Certain Nike-sponsored athletes were given prototype models of a shoe unlike the industry had ever produced. One of those athletes was Shalane Flanagan, who would go on to win the New York City Marathon in the shoes the very next year. That shoe was named the 4% because Nike had lab tests that proved the shoe could provide as much as a 4% improvement. I remember seeing a big change in 2019 when Nike released the Next Percent, an updated version of the original 4% that was meant to provide even bigger gains. At that point, not only were all Nike sponsored athletes wearing them, but the entire next tier of athletes were buying them, and wearing them as well. It really hit the fan in 2020 when Nike released the Alphafly, yet another update in the line, and simply offered them up for free to any athlete that wanted them at the 2020 Olympic Trials Marathon. Hundreds took them up on the offer. In the men's race, 10 of the top 12 finishers were wearing them. NAZ Elite's Scott Fauble was 12th. In the women's race, fortunately for us, most of the top competitors were sponsored by other brands and thus were not wearing the Alphaflys. NAZ Elite athletes finished first, sixth, and eighth in that race.

super shoe...except for HOKA.[4] Our athletes were losing to competitors they knew they could beat, and I knew they could beat, who had the shoes. That was frustrating. Plus, these damn shoes were taking away one of our biggest advantages. Because of the way we trained, we were always so physically strong. Our muscles, tendons, and ligaments—after so many long, grinding workouts, and so many hours in the weight room—didn't break down at the end of races. We were willing to push the envelope in training the aerobic system like few others. But now, because of the shoes, no one was breaking down at the end of races...and everyone was pushing the envelope in training. Athletes were running personal bests by several minutes in the marathon. Athletes were taking off with reckless abandon at the beginning of shorter road races, and not having to pay the price. Essentially the shoes were doing a large percentage of the work that the feet, and the lower legs, used to have to take on. As much as I tried not to let the whole thing bother me, it was bothering me...a lot. And it was causing me to re-think all of the training principles I believed in so deeply, the same principles that had brought us such success.

---

[4] What makes a super shoe truly super is not the carbon fiber plate that's inserted into the midsole foam. That gets talked about a lot, but that's actually only a very small part of it. The super part is the midsole foam itself. The material that's being used is called polyether block amide (PEBA) and the combination of its physical properties make it the most responsive foam ever used in a running shoe...and it's not close. Add to that the geometry of the shoes that includes a larger stack height in the heel and forefoot than traditional racing shoes, thus encouraging/amplifying a rocking motion that takes the energy from the foot strike and sends it forward, essentially catapulting the foot off the ground with each step...and abracadabra...you have a super shoe.

In addition to the shoes, there was what I've come to call the Ingebrigtsen factor. On May 27, 2017, a 16-year-old kid from Norway of all places, broke four minutes in the mile. One year later, this same kid, at 17, ran 3:52.28. In 2019 he ran 13:02.03 for 5,000 meters, finished fifth in the world in that event, and fourth in the world at 1500. All of it led to Tokyo, where on August 7, 2021, this young man—at 20 years of age, won the Olympic Gold Medal in the 1500 meters. His name was Jakob Ingebrigtsen. And turns out he had two brothers that were also pretty darn good; oldest brother Henrik is a seven-time medalist at the European Championships and was fifth at the 2012 Olympics in the 1500, and middle brother Filip was the World Championship bronze medalist in 2017 and a sub 3:50 miler. They were all coached by the same man—their father, Gjert Ingebrigtsen.

Like in any sport, when a team or an individual is having success, others try to emulate what they're doing. American football is a great example. When Bill Parcells and the late 80s Giants were winning Super Bowls with running and defense, the NFL became a league of running and defense. When the early 2000s Rams shocked the world by winning the Super Bowl with an aerial attack known as "the greatest show on turf," quarterbacks across the league began throwing the ball with greater frequency than at any time in the sport's history. And finally, when Bill Belichick and Tom Brady won six Super Bowls together with a balanced attack and tons of analytics, the NFL became a league of data nerds behind the scenes— valuing computer-generated algorithms over old school gut feelings.[5]

---

[5] I have always been a gut-feeling coach. I could never stand the Patriots.

And so it's been in the world of distance running as coaches all over the world have scrambled to try and figure out what the heck these Ingebrigtsens are doing and how is it working so well? One of the first things people picked up on was that they were often working out hard twice in one day. Now, running twice a day was nothing new. Our NAZ marathoners run twice a day, almost every day. Even our non-marathoners run twice in a day multiple times per week. And the same goes for high-level distance runners all over the world. But up until the Ingebrigtsens' training became more widely scrutinized, "doubles" mainly consisted of either two easy runs, or one hard session and one easy run. Two hard sessions in one day seemed crazy…until it didn't.

What we have learned is that the Ingebrigtsens are very calculated about these doubles using specific blood lactate levels to determine the pace for everything they're doing.[6] During their base phase they do them twice a week. The morning session, using layman's terms, involves about 30 minutes total of high-end aerobic work at about 2 hour, 20 minute race pace (marathon-ish effort for professionals). The afternoon session is then either a set of 400s (as many as 16) at 10k race effort, or a set of 1-kilometer repeats (up to 8) at one-hour race pace effort. Their third hard workout of the week during this phase is almost always a set of 20 x 200-meter hill repeats. In the simplest terms I can muster, Gjert Ingebrigtsen was maximizing the time his boys spent in the training zones where

---

[6] https://insiderunningpodcast.podbean.com/e/218-kristian-from-norway-returns/

athletes can make the biggest physiological gains and turning them into aerobic machines.[7]

My own introduction to this type of training came a lot closer to home. Mike Smith, the head coach of the Northern Arizona University Lumberjacks, had begun incorporating double sessions into his collegiate system somewhere around 2020 and, like for the Ingebrigtsens, it was clearly working. Mike had already led his men's team to NCAA cross country titles in 2017 and 2018 before even trying these doubles so it's not as if he didn't know what he was doing before. And I have no idea if it was the Ingebrigtsens' success that led him to try this new training out or not. Mike and I are friends, I've known him since 2007, but we don't really talk shop. We talk about culture and mindset sometimes, but not the nitty gritty of training. He keeps that pretty close to the vest, which is totally fine.

Anyway, and perhaps I wasn't looking close enough, there was nothing that NAU accomplished before 2020 that really surprised me. I knew Mike was a hell of a coach and motivator and that he could get his athletes to run through a brick wall for him. I also knew Flagstaff was the best place to train in the country and that he knew how to take advantage of that. His guys were doing threshold runs at Buffalo Park, getting super strong, and using that strength to smash their opponents into oblivion on the cross country course. Seemed like a pretty simple equation to me. But then,

---

[7] I should note that the Ingebrigtsens do other workouts that are more competition specific as their peak races approach, but they are more secretive about the details of those particular sessions.

starting in 2020, there was a change. That winter, before the pandemic, the NAU men ran some times on the indoor track that blew me away. Tyler Day, who thankfully joined NAZ after college, ran 13:16.95 for 5,000 meters—a then American collegiate record. Luis Grijalva, just a junior at the time, ran 7:43.73, and his teammate Geordie Beamish was just a tick back in 7:44.67. I remember that being the first time where I asked myself, "What are they doing?"

And I kept asking myself that question into 2021 as Mike's athletes, his collegians at NAU, but also the handful of post-collegiate athletes he was working with, were posting these amazing marks left and right. It was at that time that I knew athletes like Luis, and Mike's wife Rachel, were doing double sessions. Luis, in particular, was doing things in training I had once thought impossible. By the summer of 2021, at the Olympic Trials, I had come to believe that Mike was the best coach in the United States—and one of the best coaches in the world. Hard as it is to say, I thought he was better than me (at least when it came to the track). And yet, I can say it because in the end, that was a helpful thing to acknowledge. It essentially gave me two choices; I could go back to the drawing board and study every single aspect of 1500 to 10,000 meter training that was out there and try to become an expert on the latest and greatest methodologies, or I could find someone else to do all that and I could focus on bringing NAZ into the modern world of professional sports. I was never much for studying when I was in school, so I quite easily chose the latter.

Here we are now, just over a year removed from those Olympic Trials and it has all worked out perfectly—to use the same phrase Steph uttered in chapter 2.0. The athletes that chose to leave NAZ are doing really well, I'm happy for them, and our culture and team vibe is a thousand times better than it was last fall. HOKA came through in a big way and not only produced a super shoe (the Rocket X 2), but one that I believe may actually be the best one out there. Steph was the first HOKA athlete to compete in it, which she did at the Boston Marathon and she said it was the best she's ever felt, hands down, in the final miles of a marathon. Aliphine wore it when she won the USATF 25k Championships in May and matter-of-factly said that she'd have won the Pittsburgh Half Marathon two weeks earlier if she'd have worn them then. And now, every single one of our athletes has them—a great sign as we look toward 2023 and beyond. Meanwhile, more and more information continues to leak out about the Ingebrigtsens' training methods, and where they came from, and Alan is incorporating much of what he's learned into our training at NAZ.[8] It is my strong belief that very soon, Alan, like Mike Smith, will be considered one of the best coaches in the world.

Finally, I'll get to quench my competitive thirst by meeting all the various business-related challenges I've set for myself and for our organization, while still talking training with Alan and Jenna here and there. Figuring out the puzzle that is marathon training is the one thing that still interests

---

[8] A Norwegian athlete named Marius Bakken was training this same way in the late 90s and early 2000s. http://www.mariusbakken.com/the-norwegian-model.html

me on the coaching side. I anticipate being a part of conversations about that event for our NAZ athletes for many years to come. And in the short term, I get to be heavily involved in one last marathon training segment for Steph—one that at the moment is going quite well.

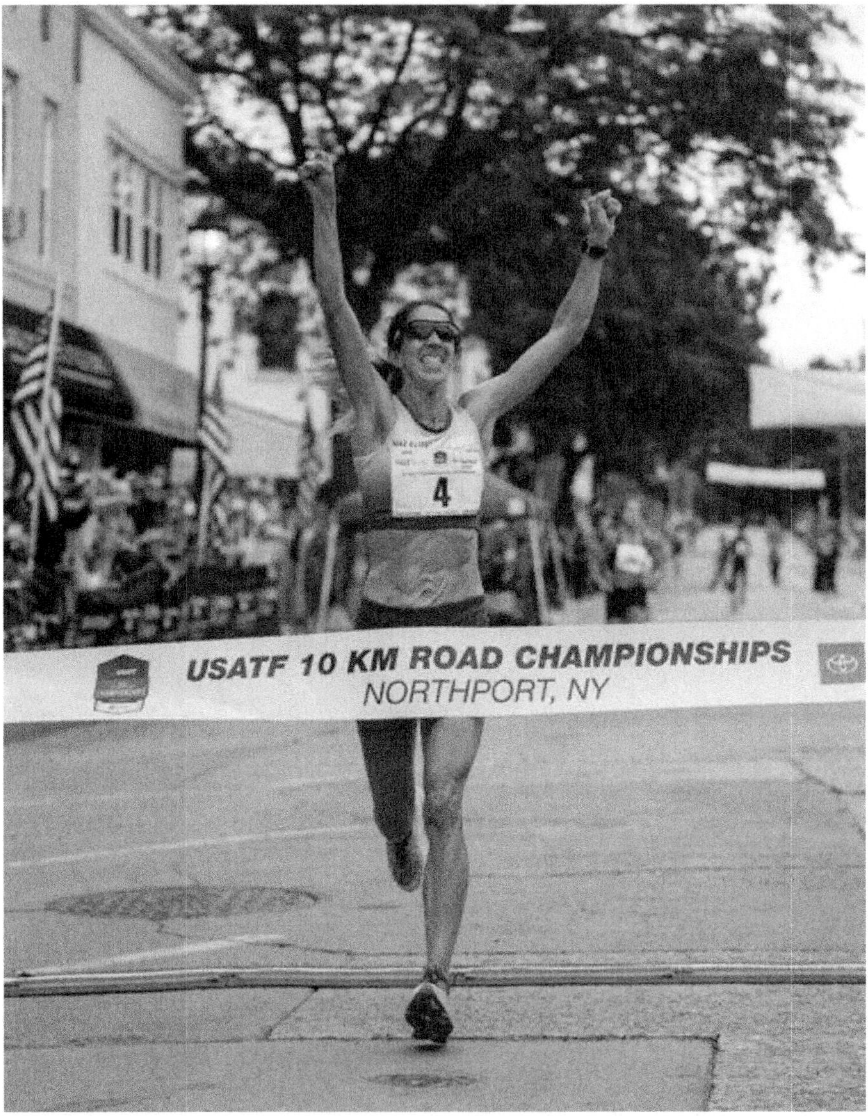
USATF 10 KM ROAD CHAMPIONSHIPS
NORTHPORT, NY
4

CHAPTER 5.0

We Finally Did It Mom

8 WEEKS OUT FROM THE NYC MARATHON
SEPTEMBER 12TH – 18TH

Joan Powelski was born in 1947 in Queens, New York and grew up in Massapequa Park on the south shore of Long Island.[1] She met James Rothstein, who grew up in Brentwood, when they were both teenagers but nothing came of it at first. They became closer friends in their early 20s but both married other people. Years later, as those marriages were ending, Joan and James found each other once again, realized they had much more

---

[1] She never lost that Long Island accent.

than a friendship, and eventually married. Joan brought two children from her previous marriage into her new life with James, Steph's brothers Terry and John. Then Joan and James had two children of their own: another boy, Jamie, and Joan's one and only daughter, Stephanie.

When Steph was a sophomore in high school, Joan faced her first battle with cancer. Specifically, she was diagnosed with cancer of the lymph nodes surrounding the carotid artery. Though she and James were divorced by this time, they had remained close and James, fighting his own battle with cancer at Memorial Sloan Kettering Cancer Center in Manhattan, insisted Joan fly from her home in Arizona back to New York to be treated. She did. Stephanie, a teenager, had her Nana move in with them while Joan was in NY.

I don't remember [that time] very well. I don't know if that's a coping mechanism or just that I was 15, 16 years old and I was concerned with partying with my friends in high school. I stayed with my grandma, and my brothers were all out of the house. I do remember talking to my mom pretty often when she was at Memorial Sloan Kettering. I would just check in. As a kid you don't understand the magnitude of what she must've been going through. She was telling me, 'I can't swallow. Food doesn't taste good. My taste buds are burnt from radiation.' She would lose her voice pretty much every other week. So she'd be talking very raspy. For me it was my mom. I didn't care what she sounded like. I was just listening to her.

Now, as an adult, having experienced trauma and grief, I'm thinking if I was talking to Riley and Hudson and they were older, and I'm going through this, I would think, 'What a weight I'm putting on my children.' But it's amazing how my mom was just like, 'Stephanie can handle this.' She never held anything back. She would never hide anything from me. You could almost see parents wanting to protect their children from what was going on but it was like, 'Nope, your dad's getting prostate cancer treatment. I'm getting cancer treatment. And this is life.'

I'm grateful for that. I honestly believe it's why I have a lot of strength and I'm able to deal with difficult things that have happened in my life. It's probably because of what I went through as a child, even though I did not understand it while I was going through it.

Things were really tough for Joan after James passed away. James remarried Maryanne Paccione, who became like another mom to Stephanie. They have remained close these last 20 years with Maryanne being very pivotal in Stephanie's childhood, teenage years, and after her father's passing. When James was gone, for Joan, it was as if she had no one. No one to lean on. Steph laments that time in her mom's life.

I never saw my mom date again. She never really got close to anyone. I don't know if that was simply because she loved my dad so much. Their marriage didn't work out and then he died. Maybe it was a protection mechanism. But as a grown woman and adult, it's sad to think, if I was 50, 'I'm going to spend the next 25 years of my life alone.' She would say things like, 'I was a great catch,' but it's a shame she couldn't share that with anyone.

Don't get me wrong. [Those years] weren't a waste. She was so happy being our mother, but I love this quote from a Glennon Doyle book, 'The greatest burden a parent can leave on a child is that of a life unlived.'[2] Meaning children can feel when their parent is not living their own life, and they're just existing to be your parent. In a way she taught me that that's never what I want. And I think that's helped me go after my own goals. I want to live my life fully and know I'm a parent but I'm also a woman, a wife, a friend.

The reality of being a parent, however, regardless of your own ambitions, is that you do have to provide for your children. After James' death, Joan took a number of odd jobs to make ends meet. She booked cruises for Norwegian Cruise Lines. She spent some time as a travel agent. She even had a paper route at one point, working from 1:00 a.m. to 3:00 a.m. as a second job. For a brief period when Steph was in high school, she and Joan actually worked together.

We were both servers. We worked for a catering company where, I don't even know what you would call it–independent I guess, they would just call us and say you need to show up for this banquet. We would dress the same, and we would show up. I remember being like, 'Okay, this is what we're doing.' And she was so cavalier about things. We'd be in the back and she'd ask me, 'Do you want some of this lemonade?' [laughing] And I'd be like, 'I don't think we can have this.' Classic Joan.

---

[2] Technically the quote is from Glennon Doyle's book, *Untamed*, "There is no greater burden on a child than the unlived life of a parent."

Joan's final years were spent as a grandparent, spoiling her six grandkids, like any good grandma should. She loved the times when the whole family was together and she could sit back and enjoy what she had created. She thrived on being the matriarch of the Rothstein clan. And Steph enjoyed being able to share her first years as a parent with Joan.

I feel like I got lucky, but in a sad way, when she was first diagnosed with breast cancer. Because I was a professional runner, I had the most flexible schedule out of all of my siblings. So we actually had a meeting with all of my brothers and we said I think mom should come up to Flagstaff. So she had surgery, a double mastectomy, down in Phoenix and then we moved her up here. She lived with us for six to nine months in 2017 and I was kind of her nurse. She had to heal from the surgery. I had to dress and undress the wounds. And I do not love hospital or medical stuff. I get grossed out. So it was a big growth moment for me to be able to see all the stuff that was going on with her.

She had a very positive attitude though. She never liked to say, 'I'm battling cancer.' It was always, 'I love cancer away.' And we were like, 'Okay, Mom.' What was really cool was that the boys were two and three at that time so they got to live with her. And there were just a lot of simple moments. She loved getting them McDonald's Egg McMuffins. So after a few weeks, every Saturday morning it was, 'Are we getting Egg McMuffins?' They expected that. And then just cuddling on the couch, which I have a lot of pictures of her, Riley, and Hudson reading together, in her lap. It's funny how kids will act so differently with their grandparents. They'll never sit in my lap and read, but with Grammy they would just be all-in.

16 months after her death, Joan is still in Steph's thoughts daily and she's a driving force behind Steph's desire to succeed in her final year as a pro.

I can talk about her and be like, 'I'm not going to cry today.' But then something will happen and I'll just have a moment where I break down. So I'm sure I think about her every day but it's whether it's intentional or not. For the longest period, I actually had to avoid looking at pictures of her. On my phone, if I was looking for something, I would have to scroll through because I didn't want to bring out an emotional reaction. But it's getting better, I think, over time. But it's hit or miss. Like, the boys just had picture day, and I would like to call her and tell her about it. So it's more whatever is happening in my life, a moment that I would like to tell her about, that's when it gets hard. I'm sure that's what will happen the rest of my life. I'll have times when everything is fine and then I'll have moments when I really wish I could call her.

Thus, we come back to our story where we begin another race week for Steph, a race week Joan would have no doubt thoroughly enjoyed. Of course, to call it "another" race week is not quite doing it justice. This was a championship race week. The final USATF road championship of her career. Over the course of her 15-plus years as a pro runner, Steph has won two national championships on the road—the 2018 10k and the 2019 Half Marathon. All told, she's been in the top five ten times, thus it would be fair to say she's been one of the best U.S. road racers of her generation. Without getting too far into the weeds, the way the U.S. road championships work is as follows; any road race in the country can bid on the rights to host a championship. Every year there are anywhere from eight to 12 championships, covering everything from the mile to the marathon. Typically the most prestigious championships to win are the most popular distances: the 10k, the half marathon, and the marathon. Steph has thrived in all three. Not only has she won the 10k and the half, but she was also second at the marathon champs in 2018—a race she ran just a month after finishing 11th at the New York City Marathon.

For the first time, this year's 10k Championships were being hosted by the Great Cow Harbor 10k in Northport, New York—a race Steph has run four times. Cow Harbor has been a popular stop for U.S. road racers for a couple of decades now, but with the 2022 edition serving as the U.S. Championships the fields were bigger and better than ever. In addition to Steph, the women's race featured defending champion and course record holder Erika Kemp of the Boston Athletic Association as well as Nell Rojas—the top American at the Boston Marathon each of the last two years. Other potential winners included newly minted American citizen, Ednah Kurgat, who had an outstanding NCAA career at the University of New Mexico, and Annie Frisbie who burst onto the scene last year by finishing just one place behind Kellyn Taylor at the 2021 New York City Marathon.

For my money though, Steph was the favorite. Ten kilometers, regardless of the surface, has arguably been Steph's best distance going all the way back to college. She was a two-time All American in the 10,000 at UCSB. As a pro, she's run 31:24.47 on the track and 31:49 on the road. She's been as high as third at the USATF Track and Field Championships at 10,000 meters (2018), and she's won the USATF 10k Road Championships (2018). She's also made two World Cross Country teams at 10k on the grass—finishing as the second American at the 2017 World Champs in Uganda and the top American in 2019 in Denmark. And the four times she's run the Cow Harbor 10k, she's been second (2010), fourth (2011), second (2012), and second again in 2021.

Plus, Steph was coming into this thing off of an awesome week of training that included another solid double workout day—this one even tougher than the last. Just four days before Cow Harbor, on Tuesday, Steph ran 2 x 3 miles in the morning on a hilly road loop, averaging just under 5:40 per mile. Then she came back in the afternoon and ran 12 x 1k with 90 seconds rest and averaged 3:22 per k. That afternoon session had an epic feel to it. She and Julia and Lauren were doing it together, all three having worked out in the morning as well. It was pouring down rain as we all drove to what we call Kiltie—a neighborhood loop that's a great place to do repeat workouts. As they warmed up, and a light rain continued to come down, it brought me back to some of the rainy workouts of my own running career. Those are the ones you remember, after all. The perfect days don't stick with you, the tough ones do.

With Ben on pacing duty, Steph tucked in behind and just had a look about her. She's so strong right now, and her form is impeccable. After 25 years of running, she's transformed herself into a finely tuned machine. Though her feet still strike the ground with sort of a "marathoner's shuffle," she no longer sits in the bucket like she did early on in her career. Her upper body posture is now textbook, with a slightly forward lean, but not too much. Her legs fire away, totally symmetrical as they pop off the pavement, driving her forward with apparent ease. And through it all, from the first repeat to the last, her face is expressionless. Like a world champion poker player, she never shows her hand.

It was a joy for Jenna and I to bike along and watch it all unfold. We hung back and quietly praised each athlete. Lauren looked every bit Steph's equal, as smooth as ever, and ready for her own national championship race, the 10 mile, in two weeks in Minnesota. Julia, after a year-and-a-half battle with Long Covid, finally looks like the athlete we signed in the summer of 2020. She was the star of the day really. There is nothing like seeing an athlete overcome adversity and what Julia has gone through since February of 2021 I wouldn't wish on my worst enemy. Today was the first day I really allowed myself to start thinking that maybe she could have a good one at the U.S. Marathon Championships in December.

For Steph, with that workout behind her, it was now time to focus on Cow Harbor. She, Ben, and the boys left on Thursday—this was a race she wanted the whole family to enjoy together. I talked to Ben about the race plan on Wednesday morning a bit. He's also run Cow Harbor a number of times, and knows the hilly course well. We both agreed that the race was Steph's to lose and that she'd have plenty of opportunities to make a move. In particular we talked about the last two miles and the fact that she could either move hard between four and five on the final major uphill, or wait until the last 1200 and rip the downhill finish much like she had when she won the Peachtree Road Race in Atlanta back in 2018—her first national title. I called Steph Wednesday afternoon but it wasn't necessarily a race plan call. It was more just to see how she was doing, and give her a little extra confidence—not that she needed it.

Are you ready to win this thing?

Yeah I think so. I am just going to cover everything and make sure it never gets slow.

Pretty simple. In my experience, the more an athlete has dissected the race beforehand and constructed a preconceived narrative in their head about how things are going to play out, the higher the likelihood they'll run poorly. The way Steph spoke in that brief conversation…she was not going to run poorly.

Race morning was pretty nice, all things considered. Mid-September in New York can often still be fairly hot and sticky but with temps in the 60s and humidity in the 60-70% range, the runners were dealt a better day than usual at Cow Harbor. If any of you reading this book ran a road race between about 1975, when the first running boom was in full swing, and 2000 or so when the second running boom began, you'll be able to picture the pre-race scene in Northport. It's old school. Okay, yes—it's electronically timed, but other than that it might as well be a chalk line on the street marking the start and some middle-aged dude yelling, "Runners set, go," to get things going. And I honestly mean that in the most endearing way possible. I love it because it brings me back to the first road race I ever ran—the Run For The Hills 5k in 1993. There's still a place for this kind of community-run event, even amidst the giant productions you now see at races like the Boston, Chicago, and New York City Marathons.

Regardless of the level of pomp and circumstance, a footrace is a footrace, and the fastest person to get from point A to point B wins. So simple. So pure. And at 8:30 a.m. in the tiny village of Northport, the race was on.

I would say, the biggest factor for me was the weather. It was the first time I started this race and I was not like, 'Oh my gosh.' Every other year [I've run Cow Harbor] it was like your body knew how high the humidity was, how hot it was, and I didn't have any of that feeling. And so I was like, 'Okay, now I just have to worry about how hard I'm going to run, and if I can beat people.'

My plan was not necessarily to be aggressive but just kind of match whatever the other women were doing. But after like 800 meters, I honestly was like, 'Uhh…this feels kind of easy, no one's pushing.' So then I was like, 'Well I'm going to go to the front now.' So then I started to push, knowing the downhill was coming and it was so funny how I thought I was kind of getting a little bit of a gap and then once we hit the downhill one of the women, Dakotah Lindwurm, she put what seemed like 100 meters on us in about six seconds. I thought to myself, 'Oh my gosh, that's going to hurt.' Because it's a jarring downhill. It's actually really uncomfortable. It's not like, 'Oh, this is fun to run this fast.' It's more like, 'I don't even know how to run this.' I just knew you had to keep your legs underneath you…

I think I went through the mile, I don't know the official split, in maybe 4:55, 4:56, something like that. And then immediately, as soon as it flattened out, I went right back to the front and caught Dakotah. And then, for the first time [at Cow Harbor] I actually felt okay on that next mile. In years past I was like, 'Oh my gosh, how am I going to get up this hill?' So getting there I was kind of the aggressor, pushing a little bit. We had a good pack though, I wasn't exactly sure how many women were in it, but I know Ednah Kurgat was on my left, and I could feel someone right behind—I think that was Annie Frisbie, and we were pushing each other up the hill. No one was giving an inch. And then, once we crested, I knew it was a pretty fair-ish mile [from 2-3] so I asserted myself again...

Right before we came up to 5k is when Nell Rojas made a move, and I thought, 'Oh, this is the move,' because I forgot about the prime.[3] I guess I just wasn't concerned about that, because I was just thinking, 'How am I going to win this race?' but she made a hard move and then as we got close I realized what had happened because then after we crossed the mat I went back to the front again and started pressing...just trying to send the message, 'Hey, I'm here and I don't want us to settle at all.'

Of course, you also go through a lot of moments of doubt. You're kind of like, 'Are they stronger, or am I?' It's amazing how many thoughts go through your head. But I just kept telling myself to get to the next mile. I also find that people love the downhills, so what I would intentionally do was push on flat or up because people are like, 'I can always run a downhill,' and so I pushed right before we went to the fourth mile downhill, and that mile, with the down, was 5-flat.

---

[3] A prime (pronounced preem), is an intermediate point in a race where prizes are offered as a way to encourage faster running in the earlier stages of a race. They are more common in cycling, but some road races do insert them. The prime at Cow Harbor for leading at halfway was $500 as long as that runner finished in the top 15.

And everyone was still there and so I thought, 'This is where the racing really begins.'

From four to five I knew it gradually climbs and it's just an uncomfortable part of a 10k, four miles in, so I wouldn't say I necessarily made a move but I just started pressing as hard as I could. I was kind of like, 'I'm going from this far out,' and after a few minutes I could kind of sense that no one was next to me anymore. And I didn't look back, but I thought I had gapped people. I was running confident, but also like that 'Don't let anyone catch you kind of feeling.'

When we got to the climb at five miles, it's a really punchy hill, that's very uncomfortable. I climbed that and then…once I got to the top I was like, 'Well you gotta run as hard as you can cause this thing is not won until you cross the finish line.' I think I ran 4:54 for that sixth mile.

Then you start to hear them announcing your name but I still didn't want to celebrate or get too excited because they could still be really close and I didn't really know how close. It was only the last five seconds that I started to relish the crowd…and yeah…take it all in.

It finally happened.

From a coach's perspective, it was an absolute master class in how to race, how to override the signals in one's own head screaming at you to slow down (and then doing the opposite), and how to read your opponents—striking at the exact right time so as to ask the questions they simply don't want to have to answer.

At the awards ceremony after the race, underneath the gazebo in beautiful Northport Park, in front of hundreds of Cow Harbor finishers, longtime elite athlete coordinator Will Fodor, gave the mic to Steph to address the crowd.

I'm going to try not to cry but that's usually pretty hard for me. Like Will said, this is a really special race for me. I came here in 2010 and was second, and I kept coming back, and I was second, second, and fourth, and second, and each time I got second I said, 'Well I'm never coming back, I can't win this race.' And he just said, 'Will you please, please keep coming back?'

We stayed with our good friends Ted and Henry who live on the course [crowd cheers], that first year, and I remember my mom came out to the race [begins to choke up], and she got to watch me get second, [starts crying] and I lost my mom last year, so this is really special.[4] [pauses to collect herself] And I know she's up there watching. We finally did it mom.

---

[4] Everyone in Northport knows Henry Tobin and Ted Kaplan. They were married in 2011 after a 24-year engagement awaiting same-sex marriage legalization in New York. Henry served as the deputy mayor of the town for several years and Ted is a prominent attorney. They open their home to Cow Harbor elite runners during race weekend.

STEPH'S TRAINING THIS WEEK:

Monday: 8 mile easy run

Tuesday: AM – 2 x 3-mile tempo run with 3 minutes rest
PM – 12 x 1k with 90 seconds rest

Wednesday: AM – 9 mile easy run
PM – 3 mile easy run

Thursday: 9 mile easy run

Friday: AM – 5 mile easy run
PM – 4 mile easy run

Saturday: USATF 10k Championships. 1st. 31:52 (course record)

Sunday: 4 mile easy run

Total Weekly Mileage: 71 miles

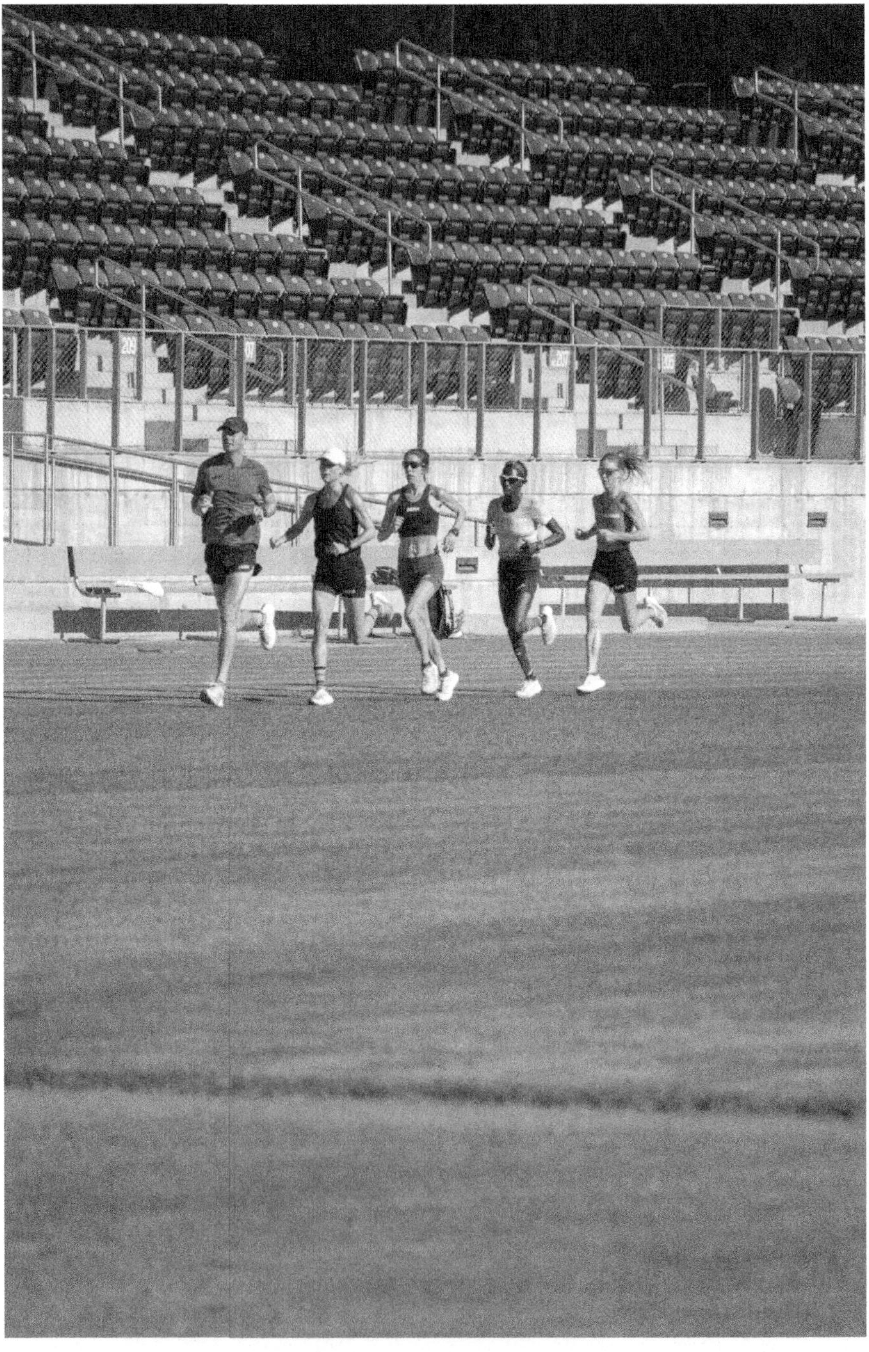

CHAPTER 6.0

Aliphine's Back

7 WEEKS OUT FROM THE NYC MARATHON
SEPTEMBER 19TH – 25TH

This week started off with very good news. Aliphine is back. Last Thursday she drove down to Phoenix to see John Ball, one of the most renowned physiotherapists in the world of running. Athletes fly in from all over the country to see JB, but we are lucky to have him just two-and-a-half hours away. Steph has been seeing him regularly for more than a decade. Alice Wright swears by him. Matt Baxter saw him last spring when he was at rock bottom with his injury troubles. And the list goes on.

It's not that Aliphine didn't believe what she was hearing from the host of other doctors she'd talked to since that first diagnosis on September 1. It was more that she just thought there was more to it. The way she phrased it was that, "I just don't feel injured this time."

With John, there's always more to it. After a three-hour visit where he poked and prodded, watched her run on the treadmill, and listened to her explain her symptoms, John felt strongly that the root of the issue was in her hips and her lower abdominals. He did a lot of manual work in those areas, gave her some exercises, and told her to continue training—but to listen to her body. That was music to Aliphine's ears.

On Tuesday the team was on the track for a variety of workouts. Julia Griffey was doing 1200-meter repeats with Kellyn in 4:10 (about 5:35 mile pace). Aliphine was scheduled to simply run an easy 10 miles. She was seeing John again on Thursday and we didn't want to do anything hard until we saw him one more time—just to be sure. She felt good though, and wanted to get in on the action. Like only Aliphine can, she sweet-talked Alan into letting her jump in with Julia and Kellyn. She was totally fine. Maybe New York City is back in the cards for her after all.

Meanwhile, Steph started off the week with a few easy days to ensure she recovered, physically and emotionally, from the big win last weekend. We also needed to make sure she re-charged the batteries in advance of what will be a big next month or so. She didn't do anything of substance until Friday when she was scheduled to run 4 x 2-miles out on Lake Mary Rd. Alan wrote the session, a continuation of his transition into the head coaching role. My feeling at this point is pretty much as long as we do the three classic "NAZ Elite" long marathon-specific workouts that remain on the docket, I am good. I think it's refreshing for Steph, mentally, to have a slightly different schedule than in years past. It keeps her excited about each and every workout, and yet, with enough of the staples still in there, she can feel confident that she'll be ready to truly race the marathon distance.[1]

In addition to being excited about the workout, she had her buddy Aliphine by her side. The visit to John Ball yesterday went well and though I wouldn't say we're all systems go, there's a lot of cautious optimism that she'll be able to get back to where she was at the end of August. Today was a good test because we know Steph's in great shape so if Aliphine could hang with her, we'd know she couldn't have lost all that much fitness. Aliphine felt the same. Her request for today was that she be allowed to "train with the champ."

The two of them took off down Lake Mary Rd. just as prescribed—nice and conservative. They hit the first repeat in 11:14 (5:37 mile pace). No problemo. Repeat number two was a little faster—5:33 for the first mile and 5:32 for the second mile. Ben B jumped in for the third rep, having paced Julia for the first four miles of her eight miles at marathon effort. He was a calming influence, making sure they didn't go too crazy just yet. They ran 11:00. Now technically, Aliphine was supposed to stop there, but

---

[1] Not that it takes much for Steph to be excited about a workout. She loves coming to practice as much today as she did when she was a freshman at UCSB.

she had asked/begged Alan to run all four if she was feeling good. Needless to say, she did all four.

The fourth and final repeat of the day was a thing of beauty. There are essentially two camps in the sport of professional running. The first believes that this is an individual sport and that athletes are better served on their own, doing what works best for them each and every day. The other camp, of which I am a proud member, says that running is a team sport and that a group of athletes, working together, will be better both individually and collectively. That running for more than oneself will produce grander, and more meaningful, performances on race day. And that battling side by side, day in and day out, over a number of years, will make the athletes on a team faster than they could have ever been by themselves. Plus, it's a whole lot more fun.

Steph and Aliphine are great examples. Either would tell you that they are better because of the other. And they would definitely tell you how fun it is to work out together. They smashed that last repeat, and even with a net uphill, ran 5:25 and then 5:23 for a total time of 10:48—faster than Aliphine had run at Buffalo Park on August 30.

I remember thinking this whole week was really smart. It's really tempting after a win to be like, 'Alright, I'm just going to jump back on the horse,' but admittedly I was sore from the [Cow Harbor] course and I wanted to respect that I was in the middle of marathon training. Don't worry that this is going to be a 70-mile week and that's going to look lame. I just wanted to make sure I got back to feeling 100%. By the day of the workout I felt pretty good. Alan kind of gave a range of what to start with—5:40-ish. We ran 5:37s on the first interval and that felt really easy. Then we just kind of naturally cut it down from there. I remember Aliphine sneakily asking, 'Hey if I feel okay can I do four?" And I'm thinking, 'She's definitely doing four.' But I was also thinking of her. I knew she had a glute thing and I didn't want her to run the fourth one if she was too tired. So I was aware of where she was at and that even though I was firing at 100%, I needed to respect her a little bit. I think it was nice, we just got faster and faster. On the last one I felt like I was holding back and we ran two 5:25s. It felt smooth, like if I was training for a different race maybe I could've gone into the hurt locker, but I finished feeling like I could do another one.

In classic Steph fashion though, this big session was only a small part of her day. She and Ben hosted eight tiny humans at their house that night for Hudson's birthday—a sleepover party.

I almost feel bad because Riley's birthday is in June so typically he gets a birthday party in nice weather and I don't think I've ever been in marathon training for his birthday, and then poor Hudson's falls every year when I'm training for Chicago or New York and I'm like, 'Ooh, Hudson also needs to celebrate his birthday.' So selfishly I wasn't wanting to do a party, and I thought, 'Let's just do a sleepover.' Then I calculated it in my head and thought, 'Stephanie why do you think that's going to be easier?' But I feel like we really haven't had a sleepover and between Ben and I, I'm thinking it can't be that much harder. We'll take 'em out to eat. We'll go do laser tag and tire them out. So it was all very calculated, knowing I was going long on Sunday. Saturday we would be able to reset after all the kids went home.

And that's typical. I plan much of my training around their lives, but their lives are also planned around my training. I definitely have moments of feeling guilty, a little bit, and I don't know if that's self-induced guilt because as a mom, or as a parent, you're taught to put your kids first and that they take priority. And that's all well and good, but I've also seen adults and parents lose their sense of self because of their children. I sometimes yell at my friends when I get their Christmas cards; don't just put your children, I want to see you too. Put yourself on that card. I think that's also led to me doing things in a way where I'm like, 'Hey what I'm doing is so short-lived in the scheme of our whole life. Our lives won't revolve around running forever.' So I think it's okay to lean in a little bit more toward what's conducive to my training and my schedule. And the boys adapt really well. I think it's all worth it.

On Sunday morning, the team met at "A1," one of Flagstaff's classic long run spots. For decades, athletes have run a 20-plus mile loop that traverses Arizona Forest Service Road 518, toward Wing Mountain, then does a "lollipop" around the mountain on road 222, before climbing back to 518 and finally heading back the way you came for the last seven miles.[2] According to Strava, the loop is officially 20.83 miles long with 1,227 feet

---

[2] I should note that this particular Sunday morning was a good one for the team as Matt Baxter won the HOKA Chicago Half Marathon—his final tune-up race before New York City.

of elevation gain, and the "course record" is 1:52:41 by Damien Gras of France, with the women's record belonging to Kellyn Taylor in 2:13:41.[3]

On this day, about 50 runners showed up to take it on.[4] Among that group were Olympic medalist Molly Seidel, multiple-time USATF road champ Biya Simbassa, and our entire NAZ Elite team—including a pregnant Kellyn, a now-healthy (hopefully) Aliphine, and Steph. But this wasn't a day for Strava crowns for us. Steph actually showed up early to knock out three miles beforehand, as her schedule called for 24 miles. Time on feet was the goal of the day. I rode along on my bike for the early miles, telling Steph and Molly that the slower you run on a day like this, the more time you get to spend on those feet. Molly said she was going to remember that one.

I stopped about six miles in and waited for Wesley Kiptoo who had turned around at 11 kilometers–he's just now getting back to hard training after a break.[5] He crushed the final 10k, cruising along at 5:20 pace per mile—

---

[3] This route has been run long before Strava was ever invented so I am not so sure this is the real course record. Flagstaff legend has it that former Boston Marathon champion Wesley Korir ran it in closer to 1:50 before the 2011 Chicago Marathon.

[4] At any one time, there are more than a hundred high level athletes training in Flagstaff, from all over the world. Some call Flagstaff home year-round and some come for month-long stints. For most of the week those teams and athletes do their own thing, but often on Sundays they come together for a long run. It's one of the coolest things about training in this amazing town.

[5] Wesley likes his mileage to be written in Ks and Alan obliges.

talking for much of the way. Mark my words; this guy is going to be one of the best marathoners in the world someday soon.[6]

Aliphine, still a little antsy to get back into shape (not that she's really that out of shape), ran ahead of Steph in a group with Julia and a few others. Steph hung back with Molly who turned early, still coming back after an injury that had forced her out of this summer's World Championships. That left Steph all alone for the final 16 miles, alone with her thoughts, which as they often do, turned to her mom. She wrote the following on Instagram later that afternoon.

Grief is something I'm always running with, running from and running towards.

Most of my running has always been about finding out how good I can be. Pushing myself to my limits. Holding back when it's needed. Running because I get to do this every day. When I'm out training I shut out the rest of whatever is going on in my life and get the job done. I've been proud of my ability to run through difficult emotional times in my life. Running has been my saving grace in many ways. Last year I didn't realize how much my mom's death had affected me physically. It's brutal. Walking through stages of grief, unexpected moments of breaking down. While the hole is still huge, I am slowly finding ways to work around grief. Running through it.

---

[6] Earlier that morning the great Eliud Kipchoge had broken his own world record in the marathon, running 2:01:09 in Berlin. Wesley said before the run started, "I am now training for Two-Zero-Zero."

Today's long run, solo the last 16, I was with mom. Singing 'Country Roads' [one of Joan's favorites] and smiling. Not stopping on the run to cry. But reminding myself how far I have come since last year. Miss her still so much!

STEPH'S TRAINING THIS WEEK:

Monday: 5 mile easy run

Tuesday: AM – 5 mile easy run
PM – 5 mile easy run

Wednesday: AM – 9 mile easy run
PM – 4 mile easy run

Thursday: 9 mile easy run

Friday: AM – 4 x 2 miles with 2 minutes rest, starting at marathon effort and cutting down
PM – 4 mile easy run

Saturday: 8 miles easy run

Sunday: 24 mile long run

Total Weekly Mileage: 86 miles

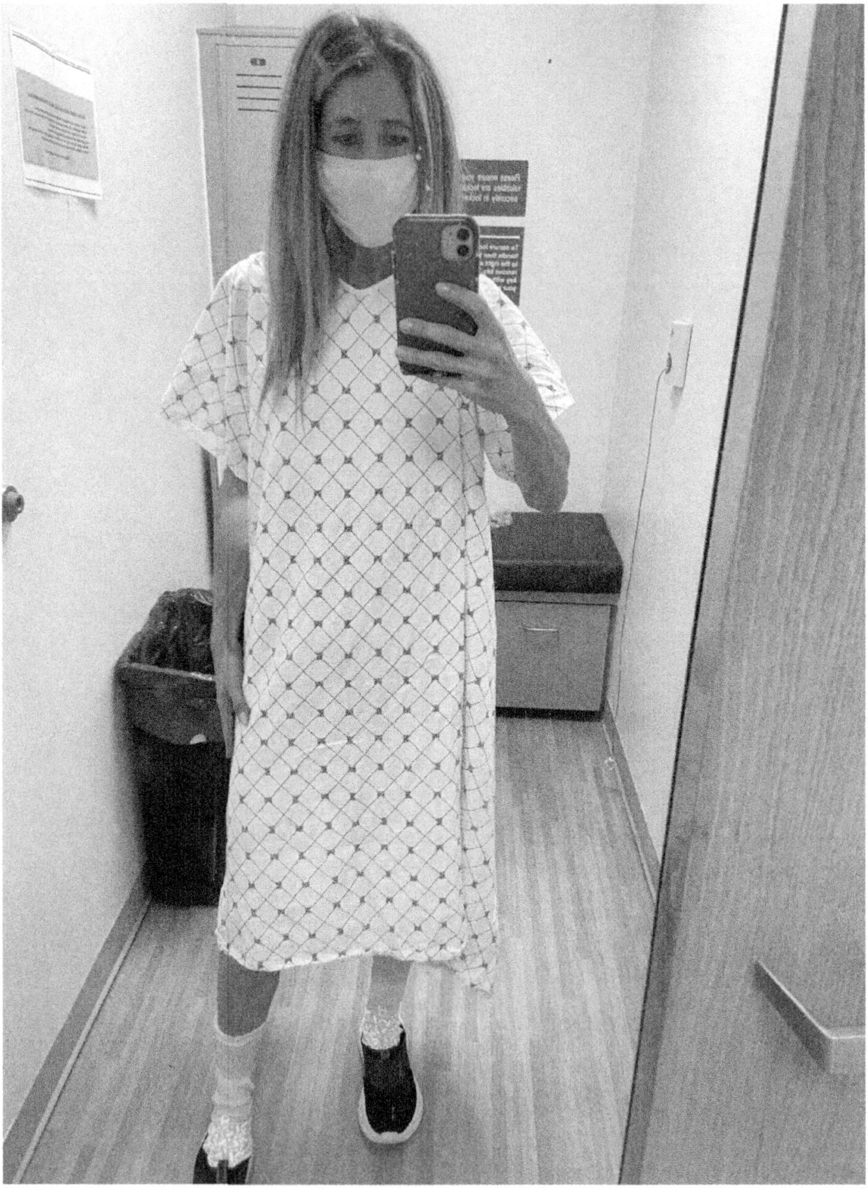

CHAPTER 6.5

Bicuspid Aortic Valve Disease
ONE YEAR EARLIER

I didn't feel right. I kept having these vertigo, dizzy, symptoms. I was having these myriad symptoms for a few months. It was also all coinciding with losing my mom. That was June of 2021. I let it ride out into the fall. I had parts of running that were going well, and parts not so well. I just didn't feel 100%. So I made just a general appointment in October here at Flagstaff Medical, with Dr. Sarah Wyard. She basically said, 'All of your blood work looks good. Your vitals are fine. Everything looks beautiful. I don't really have any reason to suspect anything…but let me do an EKG. We typically do that just to rule anything out."[1]

So she does an EKG and she says, 'I feel like I see a little something, but you're also an athlete so I'm not really sure.' She mentioned left ventricular hypertrophy, which can happen as an athlete.[2] So I said, 'What should we do?' and she ordered me an echo.[3]

They do the echo and the tech, he was very nice, said, 'I love taking pictures of your heart, your heart is so clear and beautiful.' I said, 'Thanks, I'm a professional runner.' And then halfway through, he asked me if my dad got echo's and I said, 'I'm not really sure, my dad died when I was 18.' Of course I said, 'Why did you ask that?' So now we're in this period where I don't even know if he's supposed to be talking to me about this, but now we're in so let's just explore this. He starts telling me a few things. He says, 'I'm not exactly sure but I'm seeing something that's maybe been there since birth but I'm going to send you to our cardiologist.' He writes up the report, does a script, and they get me in the next day.

I go see the cardiologist here, and Ben comes with me, and we walk in the office and he says, 'You have a congenital heart condition. It's called BAVD, bicuspid aortic valve disease. It's one of the most common congenital heart conditions.

---

[1] An EKG is an electrocardiogram. It records the electrical signal from the heart to test the patient for a variety of possible heart conditions.

[2] Left Ventricular Hypertrophy is a thickening of the walls of the lower left heart chamber.

[3] Echo is short for echocardiogram, a procedure that uses sound waves to produce images of your heart.

Congenital meaning it's been there since birth, you were born with it. And then he kind of just explains the anatomy of the heart, what the cusps look like, what a normal heart looks like, what people with BAVD look like and then he starts saying that people with this condition, since birth, their heartbeat and all the blood flow and pumping has just been more turbulent than in a normal heart, let's say. But he doesn't think it limited me. Then I explained to him what I do for a living. Then I have all these questions, and I'm really nervous. Am I getting bad news? I'm very confused.

I leave that office, and I remember sitting in my car and just thinking I have no idea who to call right now. Typically that would have been a situation where I'm going to call my Mom, or I'm going to call my Dad. But they both had died. So I was frozen, honestly. You, Coach Ben, were one of the first people I called. And even explaining it now, I don't even know what I said. It all feels very blurry at that moment. I was thinking, 'Do I run tomorrow?' And I remember you thinking, 'Do we do a workout?' It was very confusing.

As Steph took me through all of this, of course I remembered it vividly. When an athlete you've coached for eight years tells you she has a heart condition, it's pretty shocking. And it hit very close to home for me. I have an uncle who's had a heart transplant. I have a young niece with a congenital heart defect, and I have a cousin who's heart was so bad that she's had to have multiple open heart surgeries throughout her life. In fact, when Steph told me about her own CHD, my cousin was on a list waiting for a heart transplant.[4] Given all of that, you might not be surprised that my first thought was that Steph shouldn't run another step. At least not until we get this figured out.

I asked her if that's what she remembered thinking as well.

I did. That was the irrational part of me, thinking, 'Oh my gosh I can't keep doing this.' Then I looked back at all the times I didn't do well in running and I wondered was that my heart limiting me, or stopping me? Looking back now, no I don't believe so. But, I was trying to piece all these things together. That any time I had a struggle throughout my life, I was like, 'Was that my heart?' But then again, who's to say if it was. Because when they diagnose you with this you have varying levels of things going on. There's something called aortic valve regurgitation and there's leaky valve. So you have levels of where your valve is at. There's mild, moderate, and severe. When they tested me I was at moderate. But then I'm thinking, 'Have I been at moderate my whole life? Or was I mild for 35 years and just became moderate?'

I remember just sitting at home, and maybe it's losing my mom and dad to cancer, but it makes you think about your own mortality. Is this my diagnosis? Because my dad died when he was in his fifties. So is this my thing now? Am I going to die young? So then I just started to be like, 'I shouldn't run. I should have more children.' Can I have more children? I just went down a rabbit hole,

---

[4] In December of 2021, my cousin underwent successful heart transplant surgery at the Vanderbilt University Medical Center. Tragically however, during the editing of this book, my cousin passed away at the age of 43 on January 11, 2023. This book is written in her honor. Rest in peace Amy.

a downward spiral. Ben [Bruce] and I got in a fight because I felt like he didn't react the way I was reacting, or didn't quite grasp the severity of it. But he also does better with lots of facts, and lots of information, and we didn't have a lot of that yet. Whereas I'm a visceral reaction kind of person. But then when we talked it out he, of course, was like, 'Yes,' and he got mad, 'Yes this affects me, because if something happens to you I'm the number one person it affects.' That was challenging for us for a little bit.

I was just weirdly evaluating my whole life. If it ended prematurely, was I having a meaningful life? And I don't even know why I got to that point because he didn't even say this was life threatening. But I just didn't know, so I went to the worst case scenario I guess, which is not typical for me. I'm usually optimistic, glass half full. But those were my initial thoughts.

Fortunately, the initial instructions from the doctors in Flagstaff were simple, "Keep doing what you're doing." Steph was told very clearly that there was no immediate danger and that she could continue training for the 2021 New York City Marathon, which at this point was now only five-and-a-half weeks away. For me, despite some reservations, I trusted Steph, and I trusted the doctors, so we moved forward with the rest of the training segment as planned.

I think the first workout [after the diagnosis] was in Camp Verde. We were doing something pretty decent [3-mile, 6x800, 3-mile], and I remember the 800s were hard and I felt my chest. And I go, 'Is this in my head or is this my heart?' I remember finishing that day and thinking, 'I cannot run like this.' I was concerned I was going to be in my own head.

I think once I got to three weeks to go I told myself, 'You just have to forget it. You wouldn't have gotten this far if it was really a problem. They can't be that wrong at the cardiologist's.' I did two workouts in Phoenix and they went pretty well so I think I put it out. I think I went into New York optimistic but I don't know. Maybe it was in the back of my head, it's honestly hard to know.

Steph would go on to finish 10th place in New York in 2:31:05. It was another marathon that was okay, but not what she was hoping for. And she once again experienced, both leading into, and at the race itself, some of the vertigo-like symptoms she described earlier.[5] Before the race even happened though, Steph had scheduled a visit for December in Washington D.C. with one of the nation's top sports cardiologists.

Josh Cox, my agent, set me up with MedStar Health and the sports cardiologist there, Dr. Ankit Shah. Coincidentally, I googled sports cardiologist when I was looking for someone and he was the only one that came up. Whatever he did, he had a lot of recognition. He was awesome. I talked to him on the phone after the New York Marathon. Ben and I went to Mexico on vacation and on the third day of vacation I get a phone call and it's from him. It was amazing. He was on his way home and I'm like, 'Oh this is dangerous because I have so many questions for him.' But then I also didn't want to appear neurotic. I just kept asking questions. I was already asking about having more children, the risks with maternity, and I haven't even seen him yet. I guess I just wanted to put in his ear, this is what is coming, this is who I am going to be. It was really nice

---

[5] It should be noted that multiple medical professionals have confirmed that these vertigo-like symptoms are not connected to her heart condition, nor are they vertigo. As of the writing of this book, they are still a mystery.

because he was answering all of my questions, and was very reassuring. He told me the two-day appointments I would have. He had his assistant call me and basically set up what I'd be doing the first day, and what I'd be doing the second day. They were going to set me up with an exercise physiologist, one of their team doctors, just the whole gamut.

I eventually decided to take Hudson on that trip with me, just to have a little bonding partner. That was kind of fun because the boys don't separate a lot. We had explained to them what was going on. The best way to describe their reaction was Riley. [laughing] He said, 'I think I have that.' It's like the movie, *The Switch*, where they talk about hypochondria and they say, 'What's that?' 'Well that's where you think you have lots of illnesses,' and the little kid goes, 'I think I have that.' So I don't think they quite understand what it means, but maybe as they age we'll explain it a little better to them.

So I take Hudson, and he's a fun guy to have on the trip. And then Larry Rosenblatt, my other agent, or agent's assistant, meets us out there and he helps get us from one hospital to the doctor's office. The first thing I have to do is a 70-minute heart MRI. That was the most difficult one because they put you in the tube and you're weighted down. They put a strap over my head, and a weight over my waist, and they told me before that for the 70 minutes I was going to have to be doing cued breathing–inhaling and exhaling. So they would come on and say, 'Inhale,' and I'd hold my breath and then, 'Exhale,' for 70 minutes. When they wheeled me in there, they put headphones in my ear, and I think it was Sam Smith playing, and I remember laying there and tears started coming down because I was like, 'What is happening?' Even though Hudson and Larry were out in the waiting room I just felt very alone. That was when it all hit me.

But I got through that, and then I went and saw the other doctors in sports medicine, and they did gait analysis and that was kind of like a fun part. They were really invested. They're a team of doctors that I wish everyone had because they were asking me about my sleep, my life, my menstrual cycle, trying to figure out the puzzle. It wasn't preachy, making suggestions, it was just like, 'Let's see what's happening here.' I really enjoyed that. It was really calming.

The next series of appointments was with Dr. Ankit and his team. That's when I did the pulmonary stress test and where I was hooked up to everything on the treadmill. That took about 30 minutes to set up and that was the max test to see what was my heart rate doing, what was my blood pressure doing, etc. Then they did another quick MRI, they did an EKG, and then it was amazing, Dr. Ankit just listened to my heart with a stethoscope and he had me lean forward, and he said, 'Yeah, you can hear it.' He literally diagnosed me by listening to a stethoscope. Which makes you think over the years, how many doctors I had, and they just put 'heart murmur' or something on there. No one said, 'Why don't you get this checked?' It makes you think, the standard should be, 'You hear something, do this.' I'm lucky to be in a situation where I found this out and I'm very healthy, but a lot of people, where they have trouble, is they have no idea and they're 65, and they have a cardiac episode, and they're rushed into surgery. Wow. That was late.

Given that line of thought I had to ask Steph a giant "what-if." What if, when she was a little kid, six or seven years old, one of those doctors, during one of those routine check-ups, had indeed noticed something. What if she would have found out then that she had BAVD. Did she still think she would have become a runner?

With my mother? No. I think, if properly diagnosed, from what I've read, they don't say, 'Don't exercise.' They actually say, 'Do.' It will help. Even Dr. Ankit said, 'Yeah, you have this but you're the healthiest person I see.' So I don't think doctors would say don't. And wouldn't it give you an appreciation? 'I get to exercise. I get to do this.' And they would tell you, 'No problem.' So if they told my mom that, she'd have been like, 'Oh yeah, she's fine.' Knowing Joan.

The final report from Dr. Shah, after two entire days of tests, was extremely positive. He gave Steph full clearance, not only to continue running, but to continue running at a high level, if she so chose.

He said, 'If you are thinking about retiring, you need not do it because of your heart.' [laughs] Information that could have been helpful yesterday. Because I just felt like I had been through all this life-planning and changing, already, and then he tells me this. So then I go home even more confused. Because going in, it was I'm either going there and he's going to say, 'Yeah, you've got to shut it down,' or he's going to say, 'You're alright but this could be hurting it.' That's what I thought.

I remember feeling nearly exactly the same way. I was not surprised that nothing was dire in the short term. That's what we had heard back in October, or we obviously would have shut things down right then and there. But my gut feeling, or worry, was that there would come a time soon when Steph would have to stop running in order to ensure she wasn't somehow accelerating any potential issues related to the BAVD.

In theory, they say no [running is not accelerating any potential BAVD-related problems], but I don't know if he can quite have an answer to that question. Because what I'm presenting them, physiologically, he sees no issue. When I'm exerting myself to the max, no problems. Nothing's happening. But how do you know since you haven't been examining me since I was born? How do you know my heart is better or worse because of what I've been doing? Will enough people come through like me that they can do a long term study, where you have people from birth? No, because how many people are professional athletes? So that part is still confusing to me.

To that end, I pressed Steph to explain what risks she does know of, related to BAVD, in both the short term and the long term.

From what I gather the main ones are leaky valve, where the valve does something called regurgitation so blood escapes the heart, as it should, but then some comes back. So not as much goes out as it should. And that's what I have going on. Then there's something called stenosis of the valve, and that's where it's tightening. And from what I've gathered, that is a worse prognosis. Meaning when that happens, you need to replace the valve. With leaky valve, they go in and repair it. The people who don't have this diagnosed, and then all of a sudden go in and have an episode when they're older, typically that's the stenosis. The valve has just gotten tighter and tighter. That's when you hear those, 'Oh my gosh, they were walking and all of a sudden it felt like they had a heart attack.' For me, they are looking for when I go from moderate to severe. When that [regurgitation] is really happening a lot. When it gets too severe, that's when they would talk about doing surgery.

As you read all of this, like I did when I listened to Steph recount this entire period, you are probably thinking, "Are the doctors absolutely sure that the leaky valve isn't in any way related to the dizzy feelings she's had in training and in racing?" I asked her and she said no. And she's asked them, believe me. So we have to trust the doctors.

I then had just one final question, "It's almost like you had to come to peace with the possibility of retirement before that visit to Dr. Shah. But this was a pretty good case scenario. And now you've got all of this information. So how did this information, or did it not, lead to the decision to retire?"

It was almost like, when I look back now, I almost thought I had to make a decision. Because I got all this information about my heart, and I kind of have an answer as to why I was feeling that way [in the summer of 2021] but it's actually not related. I think, because of losing my mom that year I don't think I ran well in 2021 so I thought I was getting worse in running. I had a combination of everything pointing toward, 'Maybe this is what you should do.' And so then I made that decision. And I feel like I'm sitting here different, a different person than the person that made that decision. And I don't necessarily know why. And I don't know what led me to make that decision. But I'm here, and I made it. That's just where we're at.

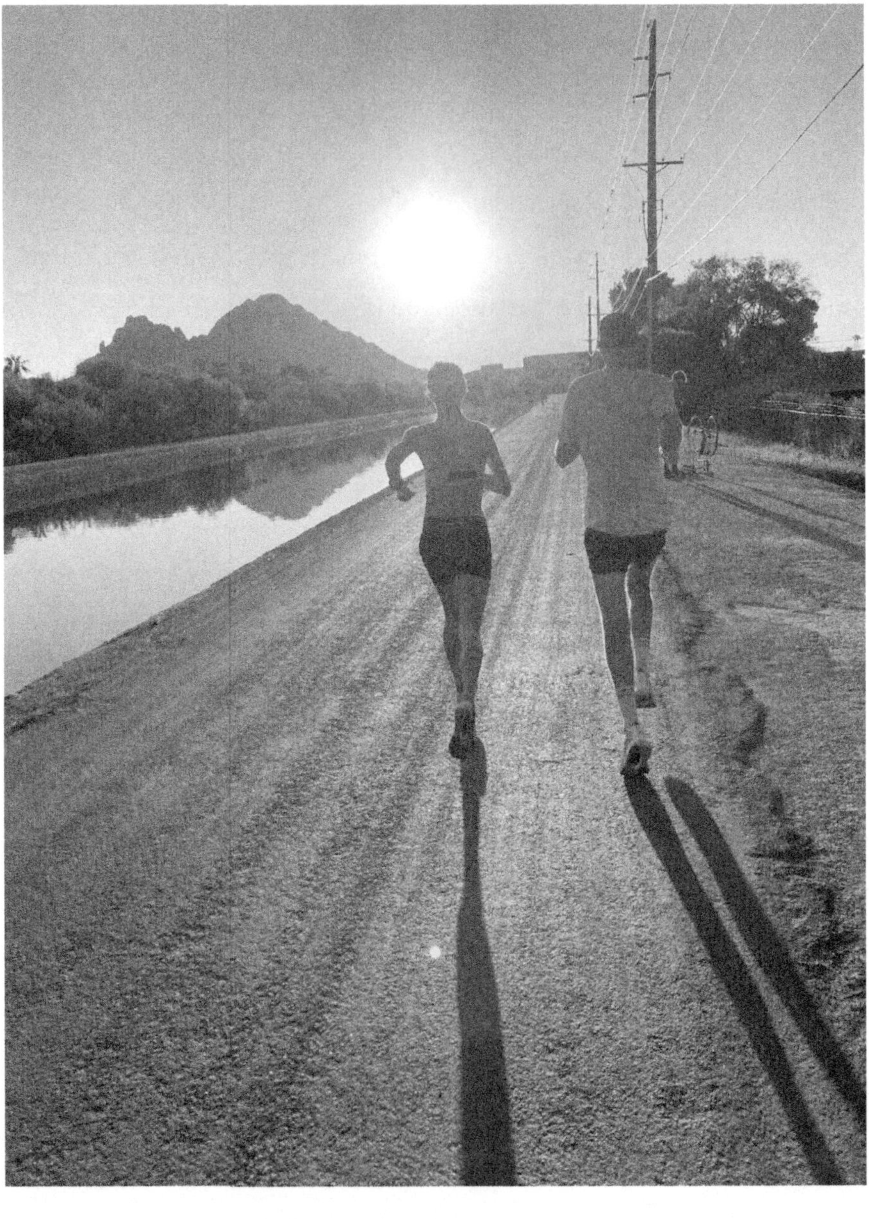

CHAPTER 7.0

Solid Gold

6 WEEKS OUT FROM THE NYC MARATHON
SEPTEMBER 26TH – OCTOBER 2ND

Six weeks out from the marathon marks the beginning of a very important period of time. In my experience, and now in my opinion, six weeks out, five weeks out, four weeks out, and three weeks out will ultimately decide your fate on race day. As a coach, if you prescribe the right work during this time, and if the athlete executes that work properly, and if they stay healthy, you really should have no reason to expect anything less than a great race. Hence, we are in somewhat of an emergency situation with

Aliphine. She worked out twice last week and did a long run on Sunday. That brought us to six weeks out. If this next month goes well, I still believe she can have a special day in New York City.

She feels that way too, but is lacking full confidence that it will happen. I think that's part of why, after doing a double workout on Tuesday, she begged the coaching staff to allow her to race this Sunday at the USATF 10 Mile Championships in Minneapolis. I spoke to both Alan and Jenna and we all felt the same way; we understood why a race could give her some confidence (if it went well), but we were concerned about interrupting the flow of training so soon after getting back into it, and more so, we were worried about the risk of re-aggravating her injury in such an uncontrolled environment. In the end, we acquiesced and told her we were behind her 100 percent. And by race day, I think that was true. A healthy coach/athlete relationship at the professional level, or any level, requires trust to go both ways. Aliphine laid out her reasons for wanting to race, they were sound, and so on we went.

Steph did that Tuesday double session with Allie and it was easy peasy. They knocked out 8 x 800 meters in the morning on the track in 2:38 per rep with 75 seconds rest. That's threshold pace for them. A pregnant Kellyn even did most of the workout, though to be fair Kellyn isn't your typical pregnant lady. I must confess that I've already begun picturing her at the 2024 Olympic Trials. Good luck to her competitors. I'll say that.

The afternoon session that day was a controlled five-mile tempo run. Steph and Allie had no issue with it. Their splits were 5:56, 5:37, 5:35, 5:37,

5:26. On average, I'd say this was marathon effort for them.[1] The ease with which they ran was part of what gave Aliphine the belief that she was ready to race on Sunday. For Steph, I think it was just a checkbox kind of day. She hit both workouts, felt good…on to the next.

And the next one was a doozy. On Saturday she was tasked with what we call the tempo/long/tempo—an 18-mile workout that starts with four miles at marathon effort, straight into 10 miles at about a minute slower than that effort but with miles 3, 6, and 9 at marathon effort or slightly faster, straight into four more miles at marathon effort. I first heard of this workout from Ryan Vail, a 2:10 marathoner who trained under Oklahoma State University's Dave Smith. We've tweaked it over the years, but the basic idea came from Dave and Ryan. Today's version was tweaked again, mostly because Steph was doing it at sea level. She was down in Phoenix because she had her 20-year high school reunion later that afternoon.[2] I am confident none of her classmates did quite this much exercise on this particular morning. Alan and I were once again on the exact same page, electing to keep the majority of the 10-mile middle portion of the run at 6:30 per mile (the same pace we were going to run at altitude) in order to ask a little more out of the three "surge" miles within. For those, we wanted 5:20s to mimic the violent pace changes that can often be inserted in New York.

---

[1] They ran this session at 6,500ft elevation.

[2] Subtle reminder that Steph is doing all this amazing training at 38 years of age.

Ben was on pace duty and I was on the bike so Steph had plenty of support. Steph had gone down the day before to relax at the condo she and Ben own not far from where she grew up in central Phoenix. Ben and I drove down together that evening, and talked about baseball for pretty much the entire two-plus hour drive. I love the fact that his boys are baseball fanatics. It reminds me of what I was like at their age, memorizing the lineups of all the teams, mimicking the batting stances of my favorite players, and studying the standings each and every day of September as the pennant races reached their climax. We arrived at the condo just before 9:00 p.m. and went straight to bed. We were set to head out the door at 6:00 a.m. sharp.

Steph is meticulous about her preparations for each and every workout, but especially one as specific as this. She had me pick up some salt tablets from the local running store on Friday because she wanted to try them out during this session. Her fueling and subsequent GI issues have been the biggest obstacle for her in her marathon career.[3] We have tried so many different approaches, but this time around simple is the name of the game. At least as of right now, she's planning on taking a couple of gels and water and salt during New York. That's it. She'll do that exact same thing today but she'll get the salt from the tablets as opposed to mixing salt into her

---

[3] GI meaning gastrointestinal. Basically the nice way of saying she's had to go poop during several of her marathons, and in fact has on more than one occasion—in her pants—a fact she has openly shared.

water.[4] With a couple of more long efforts to go, she should have her final plan dialed in by November.

I was a little worried when we walked out to the car at about 5:55 a.m. and it already felt hot. Phoenix is a desert and human beings probably shouldn't live there but they do. And don't get me wrong, I know why. From about December through March it might be the nicest place to live on the planet Earth, but holy cow it's a furnace those other seven to eight months. Steph's used to it though. She grew up there and has always run well in hot conditions as evidenced by her win at the NACAC Champs in August. She wasn't concerned.

We drove the ten minutes or so over to the Biltmore Loop where Steph has been doing workouts for nearly 25 years—since she was a freshman in high school. The rolling loop is roughly two miles around, navigating the outer edge of the Biltmore Country Club and some of the most beautiful houses in central Phoenix. I had to drop her and Ben off and find a different place to park because the Country Club brass has gotten hip to the fact that runners and cyclists park there to run the loop and the lot is supposed to be for golfers only. I found a spot along the Arizona Canal Path, parked, got my bike out, loaded up Ben and Steph's drinks in my backpack, and I was ready to roll. I rode along as they finished their warmup and it was just about time to go.

---

[4] Perhaps I should mention that during her alternating pace long run on September 10, she ran out of her salt water on what was a hot morning and asked Kellyn and I to mix some more on the fly. Not knowing what the hell we were doing, we poured WAY too much salt into her bottle, causing Steph to spit it out when she tried it. Needless to say, I am no longer in charge of her salt water.

As I said before, when Ben's pacing I don't really worry about the splits. My job today was just to give them their fluids, take some pics and videos for the 'gram, and maybe get some gems for this here book. More on that later. Steph had decided beforehand to do the entire first four miles on the loop and then head out onto the canal path for the majority of the 10-mile before getting back onto the loop for the final six miles or so of the workout. It was fun to watch the two of them run so effortlessly together around this stretch of road that they've both traversed so many times before. There was a seriousness about their approach today, but knowing them like I do, I know they were loving every minute of it. The first four miles were beautifully executed: 5:31, 5:36, 5:32, 5:33. Game on.

As they headed out onto the canal path, a flat-as-a-pancake network of nearly 70 miles of mostly crushed stone trails, the sun had just risen above Camelback Mountain, making for an epic photo op as I rode behind on my bike. I took as many shots as I could and shared them with Steph afterward. She used one on social media, and even gave me some props.[5] It really was a gorgeous backdrop for what was turning into a heckuva workout. If there was one thing I was most interested in for this one it was how Steph would handle the 5:20s in the middle of the 10-mile portion of the session. 5:20 is 1:10:00 half marathon pace and her PB for that distance is 1:09:55. So to be able to calmly and smoothly knock out three 5:20s in the middle of an 18-mile workout, especially the third one which

---

[5] I am a notoriously bad photographer and Steph has given me shit about this for almost nine years now.

would be her 15th mile of the day (including the warmup), would be impressive.

She knocked 'em out alright. Her splits were 5:19, 5:18, and 5:22 and I can attest that she was in total control.[6] And that's the key, right. I've seen so many people overdo it on workouts and fall in love with the splits they hit on a certain day, but if you're not doing it in a way that allows you to master being fast and relaxed you're doing it wrong.[7] By the end of the 10-mile we were back on the Biltmore loop and as the final four miles approached, the tension grew just a bit, all three of us knowing that if this portion were to go awry, the workout would be a bust. As such, Ben backed off just a hair on the final mile of the middle 10, running a 6:40, to ensure that Steph was ready to lock in for the next 22 minutes.

Simultaneously, a very cool thing had begun to happen. With three loops to go, we passed two older women, probably in their early 70s, who were walking the loop in the opposite direction on this wonderful Saturday morning. By now, the sun had fully risen, temps were in the upper 80s, and there were plenty of folks out and about. But these two, in particular, made a point to cheer for Steph as she flew by. As we came upon them again, Steph now cruising along at 5:30 pace and laser focused, they cheered even louder. Then on the final loop, Ben having dropped off to save his legs for

---

[6] To be fair she was back on the Biltmore loop for the 5:22 and had a net uphill.

[7] IMHO

paid pacer duties at next week's Bank of America Chicago Marathon, they joked and asked, "Where's the other guy?"

I said, "She's too fast for him. He couldn't keep up."

Steph carried on like a metronome, rocking those last four miles in 5:26, 5:31, 5:29, and 5:34 (22:02 overall). Masterful running.

It worked out to where probably less than a minute after Steph finished, those two women were coming by once again. They stopped for a chat.

Steph, a little out of breath and on the brink of exhaustion, couldn't say a whole lot. Ben and I did the thing where we explained that she was training for the New York City Marathon. You learn over the years some of the key words and phrases that will resonate with the non-runner. The Olympics, and the marathon (particularly the New York City Marathon), are two of the big ones. But the more vocal of the two understood the gravity of what Steph was doing straight away. Turns out she had worked for many years with Katherine Switzer, famous for being the first officially registered woman to complete the Boston Marathon in 1967.[8] The woman was super outgoing, and caring, and funny, and in the course of two minutes had become a fan of Stephanie Bruce. She promised to watch

---

[8] She had entered the race as K. V. Switzer and officials hadn't realized she was a woman until about four miles in when then race director Jock Semple tried to physically remove her. Switzer's boyfriend pushed Semple down, she finished the race, and women were officially allowed to enter the Boston Marathon in 1972. Switzer remains a vocal supporter of women's running to this day.

Steph on TV in New York, and made sure to repeat her name a couple of times so she had it right.

As she turned to leave I looked over at Steph and she was crying.

Ben said to the woman, "You just caught her at a bad time." He knew exactly what was happening. This caring, loving, outgoing woman in her 70s had reminded Steph of her mom.

I saw it too.

"Actually, I think it was perfect timing," I said.

After the two had gone on their way, Steph, wiping away the tears said, "Thanks a lot Joan."

Talk about a gem of a story. More like solid gold.

A one-mile cool-down later and we were back in the car headed to the condo. I dropped Ben and Steph off and shot over to Whole Foods for some post-workout smoothies. Steph tried to pay me when I brought them in but I just said, "You just owe me some beers in New York. Lots of beers." And off I went back up to Flagstaff.

When you are working with multiple athletes there is not a whole lot of time to relish any one particular workout. It's pretty much one thing after another. And for us this weekend, it was on to the USATF 10 Mile

Champs where Aliphine, Lauren, and Nick were all competing. The race was set to go off at 7 a.m. central time in Minnesota. I set my alarm for 4:55 Flagstaff time so I could get up and watch the entire race online. I tend to wake up very nervous, in a good way, when I believe deep down that something big is going to happen. I can't say I had that exact feeling. It was more like I thought, "Well, maybe." Maybe Lauren can win if all goes well. Maybe Aliphine can win if they let the pace stay conservative and she is allowed to make a big surge. Maybe Nick can be in the top ten if he really crushes it.

Instead, it was sort of a so-so day. Lauren had to drop out at five miles due to an upper hamstring strain she suffered after a super-fast early downhill mile that the lead pack ran in 5:00. That pace did not serve Aliphine well either. It was a total shock to her system after only two weeks of baby workouts, with nothing even remotely near that kind of rhythm. She pretty much red-lined the entire way, though she did somehow manage to finish fifth and set a team record of 52:35 in the process. Nick, though I thought he ran very well, ended up 15th in 47:41. That's just how deep things are in the U.S. these days.

The best news to come out of the day, by far, was that Aliphine felt fine afterward in terms of her muscles, tendons, ligaments, and bones. Nothing hurt. And she also (maturely) saw it for what it was—a step in the right direction and a great workout with five weeks to go.

STEPH'S TRAINING THIS WEEK:

Monday: AM – 8 mile easy run

Tuesday: AM - 8 x 800 at lactate threshold pace w/ 75 seconds rest. PM – 5 mile moderate progression run

Wednesday: AM – 6 mile easy run
PM – 6 mile easy run

Thursday: AM – 14 mile easy run
PM – 4 mile easy run

Friday: 9 mile easy run
PM – 4 mile easy run

Saturday: tempo/long/tempo. 4 miles at marathon effort/ 10 miles at one-minute slower than marathon effort with surge miles at 10 seconds faster than marathon effort on miles 3, 6 and 9/ 4 miles at marathon effort.

Sunday: 8 mile easy run

Total Weekly Mileage: 94 miles

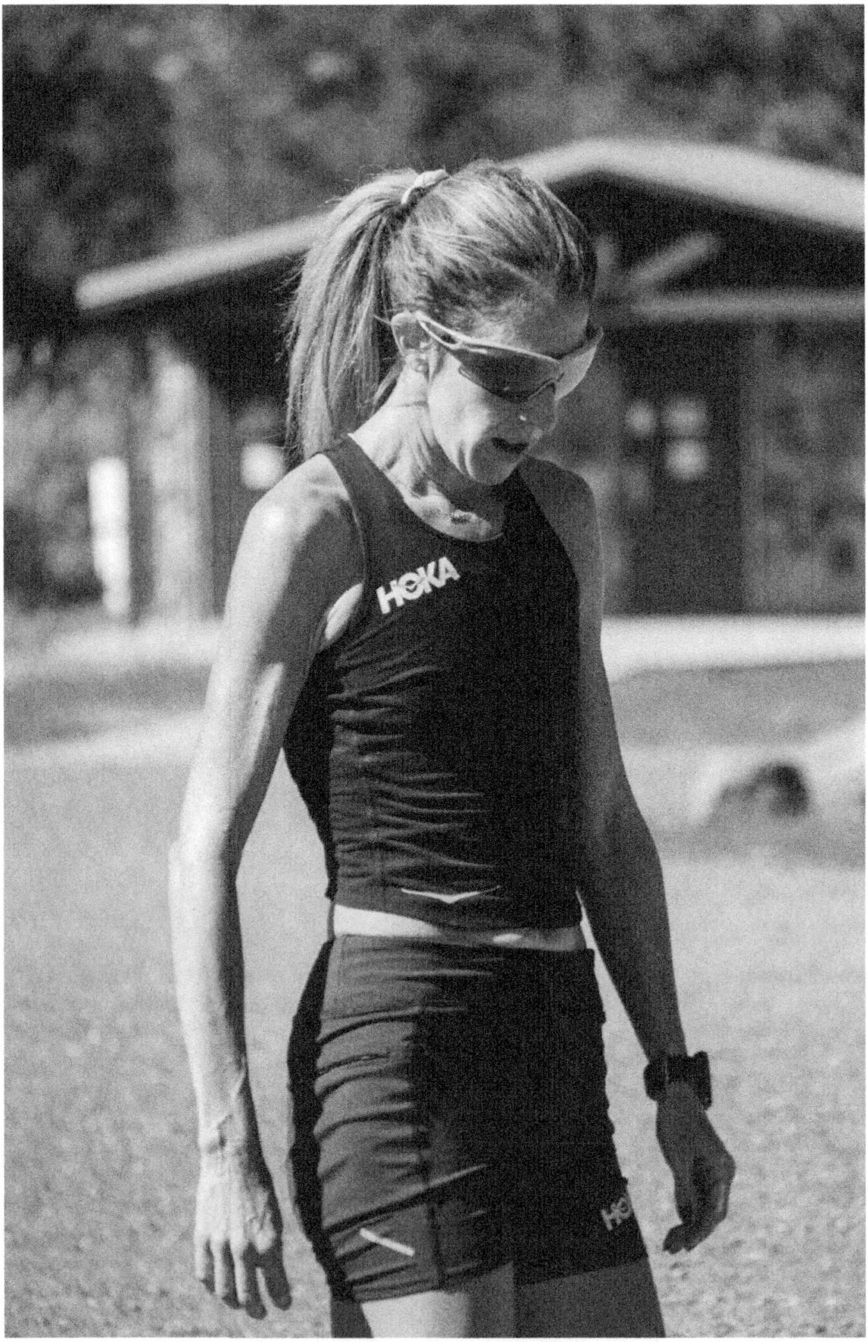
HOKA

CHAPTER 8.0

I'm Relishing the Solo Suffering

5 WEEKS OUT FROM THE NYC MARATHON
OCTOBER 3RD – 9TH

The most important stretch of training we'll do before New York continued this week and I must say it went quite well. Also, the collaboration that's been present throughout the segment between Alan and I was on full display because I think, without him, I would have done things differently. And I suppose I can't be sure, but most likely the same is true for him as well. After Aliphine's run at the 10 Mile Champs I was a little hesitant to stick with the plan of having her run the 4 x 5k workout that Alan had written for Steph this coming Friday. It would only be five days after a grueling race in Minnesota, a race that we were worried about due to the strain it would put on her body so soon after an injury scare. But he stayed calm and confident, believing that if we kept the pace right at marathon effort for the session that she'd be fine. My only addition was making sure we did something light on Wednesday to shake the legs out in between the race and that workout. She did a little 10 x 1-minute fartlek session that morning and it went well.

Meanwhile, Steph had an optional double day on Tuesday. This is definitely new for us. We've always stuck to the schedule. But Alan, rightly so, as we navigate adding these double sessions into our training, wasn't sure how Steph would feel after 20 x 400 on the track in the morning so the p.m. plan was a five-mile run with four miles at a steady moderate effort if she felt fine and the whole thing at a normal, easy run effort if she was tired. Turned out that once again, as has been the case nearly all segment, she felt good.[1] The 20 x 400 was yet another human metronome session, despite being by herself, where she locked in and hit them all at, or very near, 75 seconds on the nose with just 45 seconds of recovery in between each rep. Alan monitored and relayed that it had gone off without a hitch. Steph texted me the recap and checked in to see if I wanted to ride along for her afternoon session, which I was happy to do.

She was in mom-mode for this one and parked at Riley and Hudson's elementary school at 2:30 p.m. so she could get her run in and finish up in

---

[1] Knock on wood.

time to pick them up at 3:20. Runner moms are very efficient that way. I rode down from my house which is only a mile away and met her as she ran up toward my neighborhood where she'd be doing the majority of her moderate effort miles. She had just started picking it up when I got to her so I didn't say much for a few minutes until she just said, "I'm fine, we can talk if you want."

I guess I forgot that at this level of fitness, six-minute pace is still conversational.

We chatted about the morning and where she's at in her segment. We talked about our kids and what they're up to. I love bragging about Addison, my daughter, to Steph, and to Aliphine, and to Kellyn. She's grown up with them around as role models, and they've seen her mature into a pretty darn awesome sixth-grader who dances, and sings, and acts, and plays the piano. I'm a proud dad, that's for sure. And of course I love hearing about Riley and Hudson from Steph, and about Zoe from Aliphine, and about Kylyn and Koen (and whatever foster children they may have at the time) from Kellyn. Working with adults who have other things going on in their lives is definitely my sweet spot. I am transitioning out of the coaching biz anyway, but if I were to ever do it again, I just don't think I could work with college kids. In the words of Danny Glover as Roger Murtaugh in Lethal Weapon, "I'm getting too old for this shit."

We also talked about whether or not we should get a pacer for Friday's 4 x 5k workout down in Camp Verde. Ben would be traveling to Chicago that day so he was unavailable. We have a couple of sub-elite type guys in

Flagstaff that we occasionally pay to jump in and help when Ben can't make it, but Steph said she'd be fine.

"Actually, I'm relishing the solo suffering," she said.

We finished up the run as she neared the school and jogged the last bit to the parking lot. I asked Steph if Ben would be willing to take over the kids running program that I've directed there the last six years now that Addison has moved on to middle school. She reminded me that she could run it as well.

"That's right. You can. I'm so used to being protective of your time. You'll be retired, you can do whatever you want," I said.

"Probably," she said with a smile.[2]

Friday's 4 x 5k was going to be fun for me. As I focus more and more on my role as director, I realize I won't have many more opportunities to do real coaching. I'm sure I'll need to facilitate a session here and there but it likely won't be the big ones like this. And though I'm fine with that, it still wasn't lost on me that I should soak this one in.

I met Steph and Aliphine, as well as 2:28 marathoner, Paige Stoner, who was visiting our team this week, at an exit right off the highway at the

---

[2] Hmm. I have no idea what she meant by that, but I suppose we'll all find out when the time comes.

south end of town. We meet there in a dirt parking lot whenever we're going to carpool down to Camp Verde. The hour-long drive down can sometimes be quiet, and it can sometimes be loud, and it can sometimes be somewhere in between—depending on the group of athletes in the car. This drive was conversational all the way and the topic was Olympic bronze medalist Molly Seidel, who we had run with on A1 just a couple weeks earlier, and who had recently revealed in an interview with *Runner's World* that she was still suffering with bouts of bulimia and that the year since winning that medal has been extremely difficult.[3] Steph and Aliphine both know Molly well, and I would say I know her fairly well. It was a tough thing to talk about, but all of us were empathetic toward Molly and want her to get back to a good place in her life, and then hopefully her running will follow.

My personal take, after even more time to reflect, is that high-level athletes (endurance athletes especially) are often a lot like artists, comedians, musicians, poets, writers, etc. The same things that make them great can often be their downfall. They walk a tightrope between healthy and unhealthy obsession. It's one of the things that makes coaching so tough. You want any athlete you work with to remain on the healthy side. You want that so badly for them, and you try your best to nudge them in that direction, but there are just some things you simply cannot control. There are some internal struggles that you cannot fight for another individual. They have to fight it themselves. You just have to support them.

---

[3] https://www.runnersworld.com/health-injuries/a41534525/molly-seidel-struggles-with-mental-health/

When we arrived in Camp Verde, it was back to business. Rarely do the car conversations continue on into the workout. It's sort of like we get out of the car and it's as if the ride down never happened. The mood became light, as it usually does with Steph and Aliphine, and off they went on their jog while I drove the 3-mile loop and set out the cones at each quarter mile.[4]

Alan and I had discussed the pace for this one at length earlier in the week. We felt strongly that 5:35s was the way to go for at least the first two, and maybe a little faster after that if all was going well. To be fair, it's not like we never get it wrong. Matt Baxter had this same session one week earlier. And like Aliphine, he was coming off a race five days prior. Unfortunately, we sent him out with loose instructions to run between 4:55 and 5:00 pace and, of course—like most athletes would, he ran at the faster end of that range from the gun. The result was that he was cooked after three and we had to cut the workout short. Our fault, not his. That screw-up had us more locked in for this one. 5:35 per mile is 2:26:23 pace for a marathon.

Aliphine has run that before, and Steph is certainly in that fitness (probably better) right now—point being that we were starting out at a realistic goal marathon pace—not a "dreamy" goal marathon pace which we did with Matt. That set them up for success and they nailed it.

They hit number one in 17:07 which is actually right at 5:30 pace, but even that is only 2:24:26 marathon pace, which on a flat course like the one we

---

[4] Yes—I have every quarter-mile marked. Hitting your splits is important!

were running on would be very realistic for these two. The second 5k, and this was on only two minutes rest, was pretty much exactly the same—17:09. They picked it up a hair on number three and ran 17:01, still in total control, which was the goal. The fourth repeat, which would take them to 20 kilometers worth of total hard work on the day, did not come with a complete green light to crank it, but certainly the allowance for a pick-up in effort. And we'd just see where that pick-up took them pace-wise.

They hit the first mile in 5:29 and then Steph became the aggressor, ratcheting up the effort, and lowering the pace—5:21 for mile two. On the final mile it was Aliphine's turn, and she moved fairly hard with just under a half mile to go, eventually gapping Steph just a bit and running 16:39 to Steph's 16:43. 2:20:30 and 2:21:04 marathon pace, respectively.

I felt like I had just watched two athletes who were going to be major players in New York.

I thought it was a really good session. It was nice because we train at altitude so much, our legs don't get to run marathon-esque pace very much, for a longer sustained effort. I felt really comfortable, honestly, up until two miles to go on the last one. And that's when I just felt like I was working. I wasn't necessarily uncomfortable, it was just like, 'Now this is getting hard.' But I also think I finished thinking I could do another one if I really had to. So that was a good sign, knowing that we cranked it down but it wasn't like we were going to the well.

STEPH'S TRAINING THIS WEEK:

Monday: AM – 10 mile easy run
PM – 4 mile easy run

Tuesday: 20 x 400 in 2 sets of 10. 45 seconds rest between 400s. Three minutes rest between sets.
PM – 5 mile moderate progression run

Wednesday: AM – 12 mile easy run
PM – 4 mile easy run

Thursday: AM – 7 mile easy run
PM – 5 mile easy run

Friday: 4 x 5k at marathon pace (slightly faster on #4) with 2 minutes rest
PM – 4 mile easy run

Saturday: 9 mile easy run

Sunday: AM – 10 mile easy run
PM – 5 mile easy run

Total Weekly Mileage: 96 miles

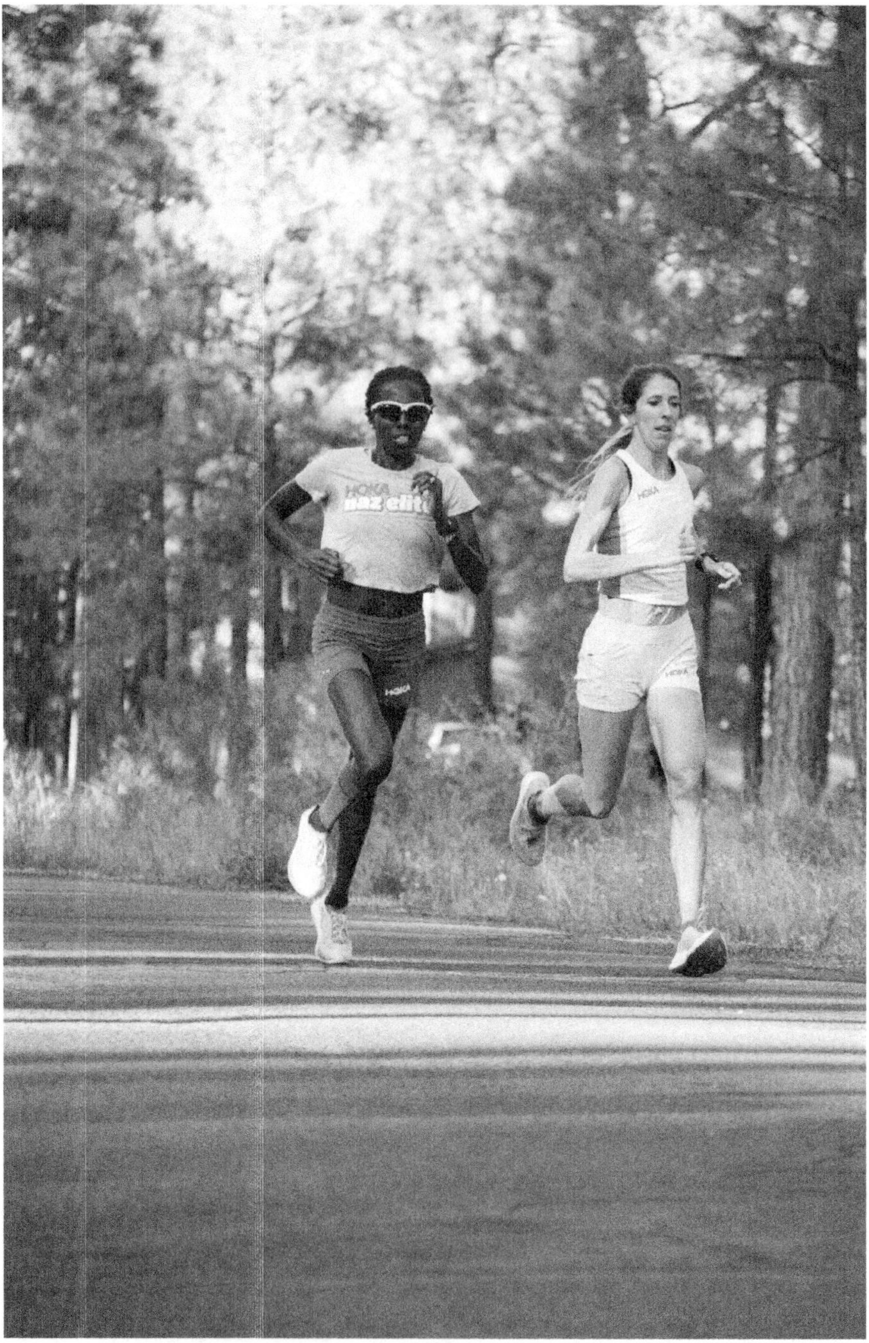

CHAPTER 9.0

Hurricane Aliphine

4 WEEKS OUT FROM THE NYC MARATHON.
OCTOBER 10TH – 16TH

This was a busy week to say the least. Because of the way last week ended with such a big session on Friday, we didn't go long until Monday which meant we'd then go hard on Thursday, and finish up the week with a tune-up half marathon in Seattle on Sunday. Coaching collaboration was once again in full effect as we had to decide whether or not to have Aliphine and Steph work out together on Monday and Thursday, and if so, what exactly the plan would be. It was pretty much a no-brainer to have them go long together on Monday. We wanted to go 20 miles with the last four at marathon effort—a session we've done many times. Being the veterans they are, Steph and Allie had their say as well. Steph suggested we do the majority of the run out-and-back on 222—a dirt road a little northwest of Flagstaff proper with fairly gentle terrain, and then do the faster miles at the end at Mountain Shadows—a low-traffic neighborhood with a mostly flat loop that's a little more than a mile. Allie asked if she could go 24 instead of 20, which was a fair request seeing as, if she's missing anything after that setback in early September, it's just the overall volume it takes for the legs to be calloused enough to handle the entire marathon distance. The plan ended up being to start together, run 18 miles, then go straight into the four at marathon effort, and then Aliphine could do a 2-mile cooldown to get her 24. Steph could be done after the fast finish—22 total.

The next issue was Thursday's session. Ideally, we'd take two days after a long run with a hard finish like that before doing something of substance again, but life schedules were getting in the way a bit. Thursday marked day one of fall break for the Bruce boys, and Steph and Ben had already planned on going down to Phoenix that day. As such, Steph had also planned a visit to John Ball—just for maintenance. Turns out, Aliphine was set to see him that day as well. From the coaching staff's perspective, we value any trip to see JB so we weren't about to have either of them cancel their appointments. So the decision was to move the workout from Thursday morning to Wednesday evening. At least that way they'd have more than 48 hours to recover from Monday's long run. Then the question was what the heck to do. We've sort of naturally fallen into a pattern where I've been writing Aliphine's training and Alan's writing things for Steph—

but we're speaking to each other before setting anything in stone. My thinking for Allie was 15 x 1k—again, my concern being her overall volume after what we missed in September. We don't have that same worry about Steph since her segment's been so flawless, and thus Alan was thinking 12 x 1k for Steph, with the last few being faster with more rest. Just the fact that, even before consulting one another, we had planned workouts that were, for all intents and purposes, nearly identical, shows how in lock-step we are—which is comforting for me. It also made it easy to decide that we should indeed put them together. The thinking was that we'd have Allie do what Alan had planned for Steph, but (unbeknownst to her) we said that if she fought back and wanted 15, we'd likely acquiesce.

The last puzzle piece of the week would be Sunday. Steph's agent, Josh Cox, had months prior worked out a deal for Steph to run the Snohomish River Run Half Marathon in suburban Seattle for an undisclosed appearance fee. When Steph brought it up to me back in the summer, I had one simple question, "Will it be worth it?"

"Yes, it's good."

"Okay, then."

Steph and I share a similar outlook on the business side of running. We both hate it when athletes undervalue themselves, and the industry as a whole, by taking "deals" that involve nothing but some free gear and then grossly misrepresent said deal by purporting to be a professional athlete, paid in socks and shoes. A professional athlete is one that makes a living, or the vast majority of that living, from their athletic endeavors—for runners this includes prize money, sponsorships, and appearance fees. Runners that make the majority of their income from a "regular" job and make some money from their athletic endeavors are semi-professionals.[1] Finally, those that make no money from their performances, and are on the fringe of making it to the next tier, are high-level amateurs. And there's a place for everyone. But Steph is most certainly a pro, and her brand has value. So when she said the appearance was worth it, I didn't fight her on going. This is her job.

But...we weren't going to have her run an all-out half marathon three weeks out from New York, that was for sure. Alan and I talked out a plan to have her run six miles before the race in sort of a moderate progression run fashion—similar to what she did last Tuesday afternoon, and then run the race right at marathon pace, no faster. Meanwhile, Aliphine would run a monster session back in Flagstaff—the tempo/long/tempo workout Steph had done in Phoenix on October 1, but on Lake Mary Rd. at 7,000 feet.

So there it was, the week was planned. Now the question was how would it all work out?

Monday was smooth sailing for the most part. The first 18 miles of the run were classic Steph and Aliphine. I drove along and gave them fluids every 5k and watched as they chatted away the miles, just two girlfriends hanging out in their preferred domain. When we got to the neighborhood

---

[1] This is what I consider myself to have been back in the day.

for the four miles at marathon effort, things got a little more serious. Steph changed into her Rocket X 2 "super shoes." Aliphine, who loathes stopping on a long run anyway, and is currently worried about her readiness for the marathon, kept running around until Steph was ready to go. Unfortunately the wind had picked up quite a bit since the run had begun and now, in a wide open piece of land with little to block it, these four miles were going to be harder than planned. We had actually done this same exact session, in this same exact location, with Scott Fauble and Scott Smith back in 2017 on their way to that year's New York City Marathon. As I remember it, the wind did the same darn thing to us and they both struggled.[2] I feared that might happen again.

But these two are just machines right now. Steph took control of the pace with Allie tucked just off her shoulder—not exactly helping with the wind, but not exactly sucking off her either. I think it was more that Aliphine just has a ton of respect for Steph and the fitness she's in, and thus trusted her to get it right. She did. The splits for those four miles were 5:45, 5:39, 5:36, 5:31. It was, for the umpteenth time this segment, a thing of beauty. Steph was happy afterward as she hopped in my car and got a ride back to where they had started the run. She and I waited there for Aliphine to finish up her 24. It took a while, which makes me wonder if she snuck in an extra mile on the day, but what can you do? With Aliphine, you have to pick your battles.

---

[2] This workout is documented in the book, *Inside A Marathon,* which I co-wrote with Scott Fauble. You can find it on Amazon!

The reports from both Steph and Allie on Tuesday were that they were recovering nicely from the long run which made Alan, Jenna, and I feel good about Wednesday. We arrived at Kiltie Loop at 3:30 p.m. on Wednesday afternoon for the warmup and it was a packed house. I felt like I needed to be there to talk to Allie about doing 12 repeats versus 15. Alan and Jenna were both coming as well, as was my wife Jen who was going to make a video of the session for our NAZ Elite YouTube channel.[3] And finally, I invited Jeff Carron from ElliptiGO, to ride along and check it out too.[4] In a way, I felt uncomfortable having so many people around. I didn't want Steph and Aliphine to think this was a bigger deal than it was. But this is just how it goes sometimes.

Fortunately, Aliphine arrived before Steph, and before Alan and Jenna as well. That allowed me to have a quick chat with her about the session. I explained that what we wanted to do was have her run with Steph for the first six Ks at 3:22 with one-minute rest, and then we'd start progressing down a little faster with 1:30 rest. So the plan would just be 12, not 15. She was pumped.

"Phew. Crisis averted," I thought.

---

[3] https://youtu.be/e356Anix9qU

[4] ElliptiGO makes what I would call portable elliptical machines made for runners that more closely mimic the running motion than a traditional elliptical machine. Jeff works for the company and has been very good to us over the years. Steph and Aliphine both have ElliptiGOs, as does the team. He was in town and had tuned up our product earlier that day.

Once the whole crew was there and Steph and Allie were ready to start, I decided I'd just stay in the car and drive Jen around for video purposes. That way, I'd leave the coaching to Alan and Jenna. I really want this transition to be complete by January, and that includes Aliphine. But if that's going to be the case, she needs to have sessions without me around. To be completely honest, I didn't love it. When I'm there, I'd rather be in charge. That's just in my DNA. If I'm not there at all it's easier. I don't find myself being jealous or anxious, because first of all I really do trust Alan and Jenna, but also because I am filling my time doing things I believe will make us better in the long run—writing pitch decks for additional sponsors, creating content for our fans (which includes this book), and working on a five-year business plan that outlines our path leading into the 2028 Olympic Games in Los Angeles. But today it was a party so I just rolled with it.

The workout was awesome. The first six splits were just as prescribed: 3:22, 3:21, 3:21, 3:22, 3:20. Those didn't seem to faze them in the slightest. Now the plan was to gradually work down from there, but Aliphine couldn't contain herself. Number seven was okay—3:19. But then they dropped it all the way down to 3:15. That was a little spicy, but how does the phrase go? You dug your grave, now you have to lie in it. Numbers nine and ten were both 3:13. They ran the next one in 3:11. And then they finished with a 3:10 on number 12. The mood was quite jovial afterward. Aliphine, especially, seemed to be on cloud nine.

Alan said afterward, "You could almost see her gaining fitness in the workout."

Steph said "Hurricane Aliphine" was coming.

I just smiled at all of it, thinking what a pleasure it is to work with these two.

Productive visits to the great John Ball followed on Thursday and then Steph was off to Seattle with Ben. The boys stayed back in Phoenix with a sitter. This was a TCB trip.[5]

Steph and I had the following text exchange on Saturday:

Me: All good out there?

Steph: Yep all good. Any final instructions for tomorrow?

Me: Yes. Remember how I said 2:24 was an aggressive marathon pace?[6] I didn't say unrealistic. Just aggressive. Run that tomorrow so we can get the data on how it feels. That'll tell us what we need to know for NYC. And just run that first 6 [before the race] like you've been doing those progression runs. Start super easy, cut it down. Average 6:30 or slightly faster. Then 5:30s for the half marathon. 1-2 mile cool-down.

---

[5] Taking care of business.

[6] In a recent conversation I had referred to 2:24 as an aggressive goal for New York and Steph had seemed a little perturbed—as if to say, "I don't think that's aggressive, I think that's exactly what I can do."

Welp. It was mission accomplished. She ran that 6-miler beforehand perfectly; with splits of 8:29, 6:43, 6:32, 6:25, 6:29 and 6:16. Then the race itself couldn't have gone smoother with splits of 5:29, 5:27, 5:31, 5:30, 5:22, 5:31, 5:28, 5:23, 5:25, 5:25, 5:26, 5:19. Her final time was 1:11:45. With a 2-mile cool-down she got in just over 21 on the day—another solid marathon-specific workout, and at the end of yet another big week. And the most important thing was how she felt. Not to make her sound pompous, but it was easy.

Back in Flag, Aliphine absolutely rocked her tempo/long/tempo. With my buddy Grant Dunstan pacing her on his bike, she ran splits just as fast as Steph had run at sea level two weeks earlier:

5:31, 5:36, 5:38, 5:38
6:25, 6:22, 5:24, 6:32, 6:27, 5:20, 6:30, 7:51 (bathroom break), 5:17, 6:28
5:23, 5:24, 5:20, 5:26

Total time: 1:46:49 (5:56 per mile)

Look out people. Hurricane Aliphine is most definitely coming.

STEPH'S TRAINING THIS WEEK:

Monday: 22 miles with last 4 at marathon effort

Tuesday: AM – 10 mile easy run
PM – 4 mile easy run

Wednesday: AM – 4 mile easy run
PM – 12 x 1k with first 6 at lactate threshold pace (1:00 rest), next 6 cutting down (1:30 rest)

Thursday: AM – 6 mile easy run
PM – 5 mile easy run

Friday: AM – 8 mile easy run
PM – 2 mile easy run

Saturday: AM – 5 mile easy run
PM – 3 mile easy run

Sunday: 6-mile progression run followed by Snohomish River Run Half Marathon. 1st – 1:11:45.

Total Weekly Mileage: 101 miles

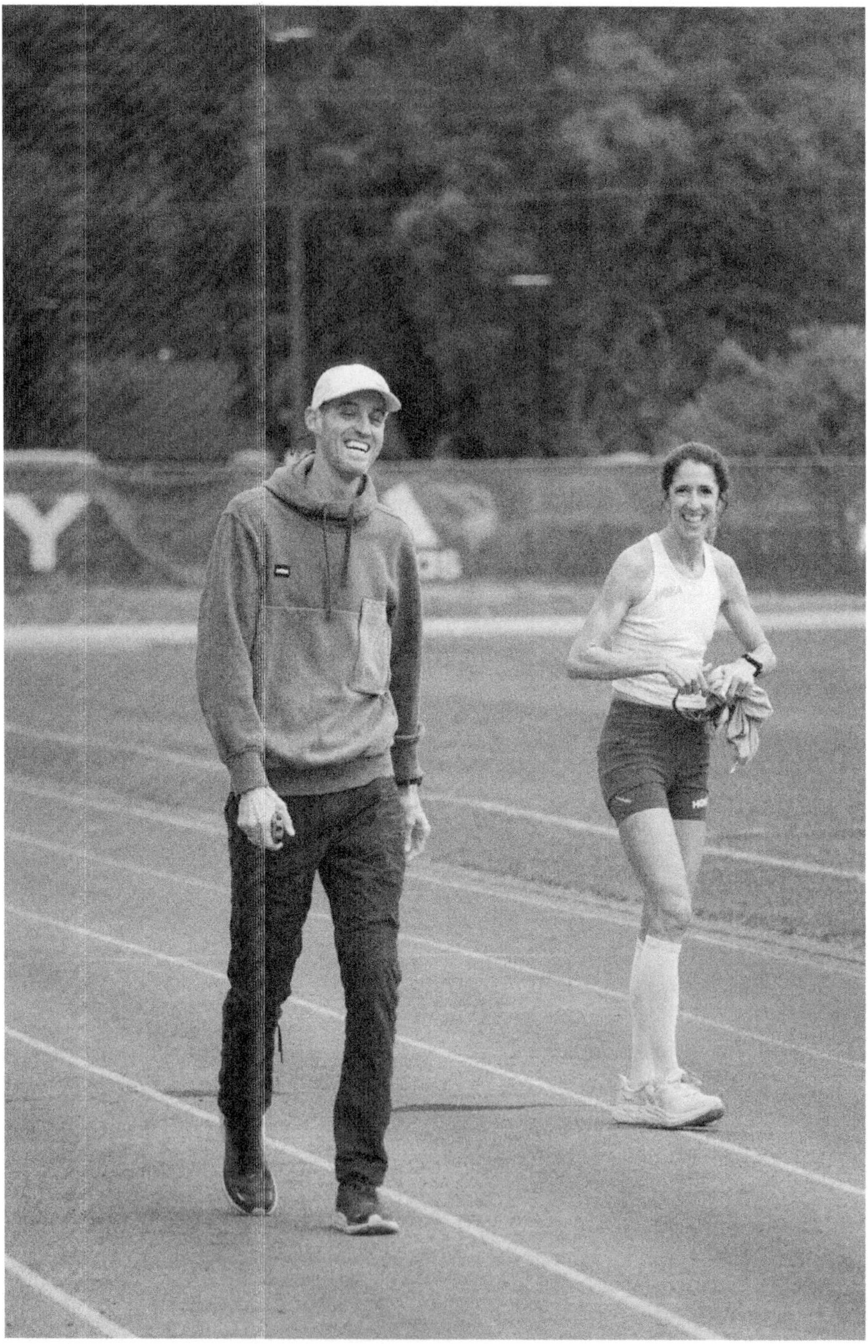

CHAPTER 10.0

Last Big Day

3 WEEKS OUT FROM THE NYC MARATHON.
OCTOBER 17TH – 23RD

"Don't fuck it up." This is what I think to myself late in a segment like this when everything has gone so well.[1] As it stands with Steph right now, Alan shares the same sentiment, though perhaps without such colorful language. At the same time, you can't just stop working. The body is in a certain flow, and it craves work. So you have to keep giving it work, you just can't get greedy. With both Steph and Aliphine coming off such big efforts on

---

[1] Knock on wood.

Sunday, we didn't want to do anything crazy mid-week—just a little session to turn the legs over a touch. Then we'd come back with one final long day on the weekend. The original plan was to wait until Thursday for the first one and then hit the final marathon specific workout on Sunday, exactly two weeks out from New York. But, plans change.

To Steph's credit, she got ahead of things by noticing early in the week that Sunday's forecast was nasty—calling for temps in the low 40s, rain, and 20-plus mph winds. That did not sound like a recipe for success. So by Tuesday we had already decided to move the sessions to Wednesday and Saturday. I wasn't too worried but that did mean that Saturday (which was going to be 24 miles of work) was going to come just six days after the half marathon for Steph and the tempo/long/tempo for Aliphine. Of course, you could make the argument that would be a good thing for Allie because, once again—though we're getting more confident by the day, the only thing we may be a touch behind on is that overall callusing that comes from the cumulative workload over the course of a segment. Now she'd for sure be running Saturday's workout on tired legs, and the positive spin is it meant the session would be that much more marathon specific. As a coach it's important to control the narrative as it relates to training, and this was a great example of turning something that could have been viewed as a negative, into a positive.

Wednesday was fun. We were back at Mountain Shadows, the neighborhood loop where Steph and Aliphine had knocked out four miles at marathon effort after 18 miles of running nine days ago. Like that morning, it was once again windy but for an easier session like this we weren't really concerned. Jenna and I were on coaching duty and both of us brought our bikes to ride along. We walked along and measured the course, putting cones down every 200 meters so the ladies could stay on pace. This was not a day to get excited. We wanted to hit the splits and get out of there. Alan wrote the session and it called for four 400s at roughly 10k pace, then six 800s at roughly half marathon pace, and finally four more 400s at the same pace as the first four. When you think about it from a relative standpoint, that's a pretty simple session for any seasoned runner. And it was. They hit everything spot on except for a couple of the quarters that were just a hair quick—probably the result of a tailwind. Mission accomplished. Mood good. On we go.

The week was probably more challenging for the coaching staff than it was for Steph or Allie. Every year, I co-direct the Northern Arizona Middle School Cross Country Championships here in Flagstaff with Vince Sherry, the co-owner of the local running store in town—Run Flagstaff. This was race week and it's typically a hassle. Registration was due on Monday, but like always, hardly any teams had signed up yet so we were scrambling to try and track down all the coaches and athletic directors who had missed the deadline. That took up much of my Monday and Tuesday and raised my stress level a few notches. Meanwhile, Alan couldn't be in Flagstaff this week. He and his wife Shayne had made the difficult decision at the end of the summer to keep the family in Boulder for another year while Alan got settled into his new job. Having gone through so many changes the year before when he had taken the coaching position at UTEP, they just felt it was too much to move the boys to Flagstaff, and away from their friends, so quickly. Plus, Shayne had a good job in Boulder and no prospects yet in

Flag. It all made total sense to me, but it's meant that Alan has been commuting back and forth from Flagstaff to Boulder nearly every week, spending Monday evening through Friday morning in Flag with the team, and then the weekend with his family in Boulder. I can only imagine how difficult it's been. This particular week he had asked to spend some extended time in Colorado, which was completely fine. It just meant that Jenna and I would have to make sure we could be at all the workouts, and there were a lot of moving parts.

Saturday was the day that was especially challenging, and it got more so as the week went on. The forecast remained one big pile of yuck for Sunday, but now Saturday wasn't looking so good either. Winds were predicted to go north of 20 miles per hour by 10 a.m. in Flagstaff which was going to cause us some issues. We felt like Steph was going to be okay. Because she has pretty much already put all of the necessary tools in the toolbox for New York, her day was scheduled to be sort of a culmination of all the double workout days she's done thus far. Her morning session would be 2 x 6 miles at slightly slower than marathon effort with a 3-minute rest in between. Then she'd come back in the afternoon with 10 x 1k at lactate threshold effort, or slightly faster. The relatively controlled nature of both workouts, and the fact that her fitness and confidence are both through the roof, had us feeling fine about all of that.

But Matt Baxter and Aliphine were a different story. Matt's segment has been choppy at best. There have been moments where it looks like he's on a path to a big run in New York—perhaps none bigger than when he won the Chicago Half Marathon at the end of September, but there have also been a number of missed days, or missed workouts, due to slight injury scares (at different times) in the achilles, the calf, and the quad. He needed a big day both physically and mentally. Aliphine's last five weeks have been much smoother than Matt's and she's so close to being in the best marathon shape of her life, but I did believe she needed one more big one. So once again the coaching staff huddled up to formulate a plan.[2]

Matt was meant to be running what we call the 10/10—a session where the athlete runs 10 miles at an easy/moderate effort and then goes straight into 10 miles at marathon effort. It was my firm opinion that we should not have him do this up in Flag, given the forecast. Knowing he needed 10 full miles before the hard part of the workout even began, I just didn't believe we could start early enough to "beat the wind." Plus, it was my gut feeling that we needed to have a day that felt good. And it's hard to feel good running into 20mph winds. Fortunately, on a day like this, we always have the option of going down to Camp Verde where it's always warmer, and almost always less windy. I have been very careful not to ever be overly assertive with Alan and Jenna, but this is probably as close as I've come all segment. To that end, I shared my opinion (strongly) Friday morning on our conference call and left it up to them from there. I never even checked back in to see what the final decision was.

For Aliphine, it was different. Her workout was a 15-miler at marathon effort—the exact same session she had done two weeks out from the 2020 Olympic Trials. After so many years together, you just kind of know what

---

[2] I cannot express how valuable it's been to have a three-person staff this segment. The stress of making these decisions by oneself is excruciating.

an athlete's thinking and I knew she'd be comparing this one to that day in February of 2020. Now of course, we were rolling the dice to an extent because if it didn't go well then it could be a disaster mentally. But if we moved the session, or changed its location, she'd be left wondering if she was truly ready without that apples to apples comparison. I believed in where she was at, fitness-wise, and thought that she'd crush this thing…as long as we beat the wind. As such, we agreed to start the warmup at 6:30 a.m., pretty much right when the sun comes up this time of year, in order to start the 15-miler around 7 a.m. before things got too blustery.

Even with Alan gone, we were able to make sure everyone was taken care of. It's been a point of pride for me since we started the team in 2014 to always have a coach, or a facilitator, at every hard workout. We are a professional organization after all. The Lakers don't have practice without coaches and neither should we.

Jenna, Alan, and Matt had all collaborated and indeed decided to go to Camp Verde for the 10/10 with Jenna driving him down there. Adding to the fun, Matt would be joined by the newest member of NAZ Elite—Futsum Zienasellassie.[3] Futsum was on the team when he came out of college back in 2017 but stayed for only one year. He left on good terms though, and I had always secretly hoped we could reunite at some point.

---

[3] Futsum is objectively one of the most talented runners in the United States. He was a national cross country champion in high school, and a four-time cross country All American in college—three times finishing in the top four at the NCAA Championships. He was also one of the nation's top 10,000 meter runners, setting a best of 27:52.70 as a senior.

Long story short, he reached out a few months ago hoping for that same thing and after a few back and forths between he and Alan, and between myself, HOKA's Director of Global Sports Marketing—Mike McManus, and Futsum's agent—Hawi Keflezighi, we came to an agreement a couple of weeks ago.[4]

With Jenna taking care of Matt and Futsum, it was on me to make sure Steph and Allie were good to go. I had talked out Steph's day with Ben B, and we were all set there. Ben would drive along for her morning workout, taking splits and giving out fluids, before eventually pacing her afternoon session—which Jenna could attend after getting back from Camp Verde.

For Aliphine, I once again enlisted the help of my good friend Grant Dunstan. Grant is really good at bike pacing (I am not), and is always willing to help. Plus, he's an early riser so the 6:30 a.m. start did not scare him off. He and Allie get along really well too, so I felt good about the plan. The coaching staff had studied the wind direction obsessively and we felt that going out and back would be the best plan of attack. I met Grant and Allie bright and early at what we call the 10-mile mark on Lake Mary and shared that we'd go from that 10-mile mark, to the three-mile mark, and then back to the 11-mile mark to get our 15 in on the day. The wind

---

[4] Hawi is Olympic medalist Meb Keflezighi's brother. After attending law school at UCLA, Hawi began representing Meb and was a natural at the agent game. He's gone on to become one of the most successful athlete representatives in the world of running and his agency, Hawi Management, reps six of our NAZ athletes—including Aliphine.

would most likely be a crosswind but with a little more hurt than help on the way out and a little more help than hurt on the way back.

I hung out as Aliphine warmed up, chatting with Grant and taking him through what we wanted in terms of splits. I felt like we should start at 5:35s and on the way back, if she felt good, she could get going a little quicker, but it wasn't necessary. 5:35 pace for 15 on Lake Mary is already world-class stuff. No need for a home run, but let's be honest—we wanted more than a single.

I would describe Allie's mood beforehand as nervously excited. She wasn't freaking out by any means, and seemed pretty confident all things considered. And her signature Aliphine smile was in full force. I remember the morning of the 2020 Olympic Trials, when she first showed up at our designated meeting spot in the host hotel, that smile was nowhere to be found. She was palpably nervous.

I pulled her aside and told her to smile, "A happy Aliphine is a dangerous Aliphine," I said.

She smiled. And she won.

Today I wouldn't be able to see it all play out though. I had to be at the middle school cross country meet at 7:30 to start setting up. So I drove along and watched the first mile, which they hit in 5:34, wished them luck, and waved goodbye. All I could do now was wait.

At that same time Steph and Ben were pulling up to their own starting spot on Lake Mary—a few miles from Aliphine, while Jenna, Matt, and Futsum were heading south on Highway 17—about a half hour away from Camp Verde. The wheels were all in motion.

As I walked the cross country course, meticulously removing any loose rocks or sticks, and marking every turn, I finally received the text from Grant; it was simply a picture of his GPS watch, and it read:

Summary
Today 7:14a
15.00mi
1:23:29   5:33/mi
Done

Boom. Mission accomplished and then some. Despite the early start, and the wind, and Aliphine's stubborn refusal to wear the super shoes, she had averaged three seconds faster per mile than she had in February of 2020, two weeks before the greatest race of her life.[5]

About an hour later I got the text from Ben B with the report on Steph's workout:

First 6 was 5:45-5:47, pretty much the same for the second 6.

---

[5] I told you she wanted that apples to apples comparison. She swears she'll wear the super shoes for a workout this coming week.

Steph texted as well, with a screenshot of her splits from Final Surge, and a two-word text:

Morning done ✓

Finally, about another hour later, the text came through from Jenna about Matt and Futsum:

5:02/5:03/4:59/5:02/5:01/4:57/5:02/5:02/4:58/4:59

Crushed it. Both looked smooth.

I have to admit, this one might have made me smile the widest. Matt has had such an unfair go of it so far as a pro. He's an amazing athlete, phenomenal teammate, loving dad and partner…I could go on and on, but he's just been bitten by the injury bug so many times. And it's not as if he's slacking on his ancillary work. No one, except maybe Steph, takes care of themselves as well as Matt does. He's a true pro. But even when you do everything right, things can go wrong. I suppose I've just always subscribed to the theory that one day all of the hard work will pay off. And maybe, just maybe, New York City will be that day for Matt Baxter.

And of course I smiled for Futsum as well. I have to believe a workout like that validates his decision to rejoin the team in a major way. The session marked the end of just his second week training with us, and he's already worked out with some of the best runners to come out of the NCAA the last couple of years in Olin Hacker, Wesley Kiptoo, and Alex Masai. Now he knocks out a workout about which he said, "I've never done anything like that before."

Welcome back Futsum.

After the cross country meet was over and we had packed everything up, I must admit that I was torn. Part of me wanted to go straight to my favorite pub and grab a burger and a beer after a hard seven straight hours of work. And part of me wanted to go watch Steph's second session of the day. But in the end, I needed to let Jenna take on the workout by herself. That's what she and I had discussed beforehand, in exchange for me taking the group that had a long run down to a spot we call Beaver Creek on Sunday morning. Like I mentioned earlier, when I'm around I sort of take over and that's not fair to Jenna. She deserves opportunities to lead without Alan or I around, so I stayed away. And hey—it didn't hurt that it allowed me to have that burger…and those beers.

So I'll leave you with a couple of more texts. The first was from Jenna to both Alan and I and it was pretty cool:

Man this woman doesn't miss a beat!
3:19/3:22/3:20/3:22/3:18/3:19/3:16/3:16/3:16/3:17

Last one was very windy

This meant that after having run 2 x 6 miles in the morning—15.3 miles total including warmup and cool-down, she came back in the afternoon and damn near repeated the session she and Aliphine had done last week that had all of us so excited. Steph herself was pumped and showed it. She texted Alan, Jenna, and I as a group later that evening:

I know we still have two weeks to go but finishing up the last big day today just wanted to say thanks to my coaches for working together and supporting this build-up. 💪

No, thank you Steph.

STEPH'S TRAINING THIS WEEK:

Monday: AM – 4 mile easy run
PM – 5 mile easy run

Tuesday: AM – 10 mile easy run
PM – 4 mile easy run

Wednesday: AM – 4 x 400/ 6 x 800/ 4 x 400
PM – 4 mile easy run

Thursday: 8 mile easy run

Friday: AM – 10 mile easy run
PM – 4 mile easy run

Saturday: AM – 2 x 6 miles at slightly slower than marathon effort with 3 minutes rest.
PM – 10 x 1k at lactate threshold, cutting down to slightly faster than threshold

Sunday: 8 miles easy

Total Weekly Mileage: 93 miles

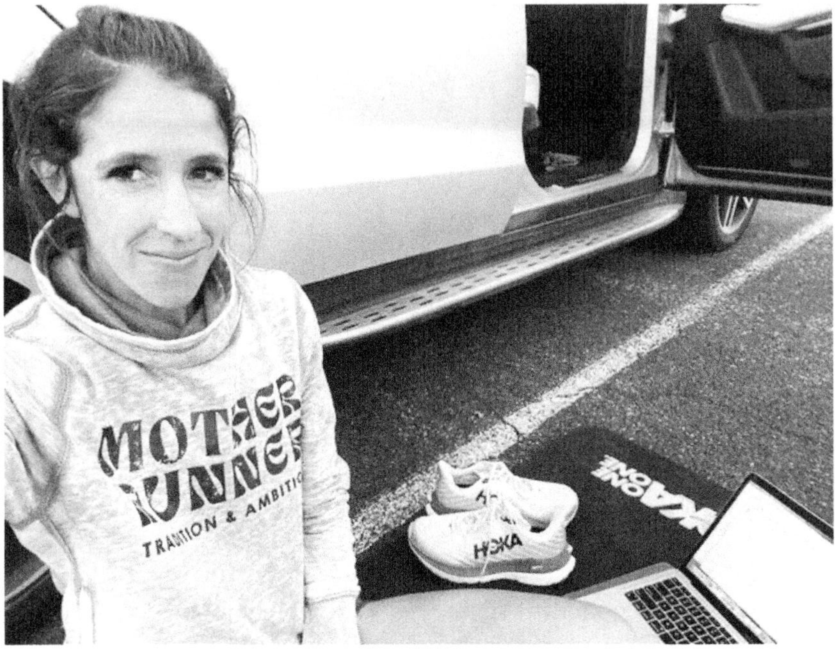
HOKA

CHAPTER 11.0

Tapering

2 WEEKS OUT FROM THE NYC MARATHON.
OCTOBER 24TH – 30TH

Having worked with Steph for so many years now, I know to expect some level of concern as a marathon nears in regards to her energy level. For as far back as I can remember, she seems to encounter what I can only describe as (for lack of a better term) "weird" symptoms during the final weeks. Those symptoms have at times included the same vertigo-like feelings she was experiencing often enough last year that she saw the doctor, eventually leading to her CHD diagnosis.[1] They have also included difficulty with digestion, mood swings, and just overall fatigue. Hearing this you may be thinking, "Is it mental, or could it be stress-induced?"

I would be lying if I said I hadn't considered that as well. When you put your heart and soul into something, like Steph does with marathon training, it is only natural to expect elevated stress levels as that something nears. We know that stress can affect all sorts of things inside the body, including the circulatory system. Sure enough, Steph got a blood test last Monday, October 17 and the results came back the next day.

Pretty much every marker related to red blood cell production was down.[2] And yet her iron and ferritin levels were high. This was difficult to understand as the body requires healthy iron levels to produce red blood cells. Steph's theory was that perhaps her iron was too high, a condition called "iron overload" in medical terminology. Counterintuitive as it may be, when the body is storing too much iron, red blood cell production is actually affected negatively and can lead to symptoms that feel similar to those that occur when a person is anemic. Because even though anemia is most often associated with low iron levels, the condition is simply the lack

---

[1] Once again, the vertigo-like symptoms are not related to the heart diagnosis, according to medical professionals.

[2] To give you an example, this test on October 17 revealed that her hematocrit level had dropped to 42.3, down from 49.3 when she was tested on September 14—just three days before she won the USATF 10k Championships. Your hematocrit number is the percentage of your blood volume that's composed of red blood cells.

of enough healthy red blood cells to carry oxygen to your body's tissues, and there can be a number of causes.

All that to say, Steph was relatively calm about the results. She still felt fine, which was the main thing. Getting the test had been precautionary. It wasn't as if she was feeling bad. And she assured me that she was not worried. We spoke about it all after she got the results and she followed up with the following text:

Also just so we're on the same page I am not concerned at all. I feel really strong and confident.

That was last Tuesday. The one immediate change she made was that she stopped taking her iron supplement in order to, hopefully, lower her iron levels in an effort to get her red blood cell production firing again. After all, the whole reason we live and train at altitude is to raise our red blood cell levels, and in turn increase our oxygen-carrying capacity—something that then gives us an advantage when we go down to race at sea level.

She described the entire situation like this:[3]

---

[3] Disclaimer: Up until this point in the book, I have been conducting interviews with Steph in real time—getting her thoughts on the previous week almost immediately after it happened. I did not do that in the final two weeks leading up to the race because I did not want to distract her from the task at hand. So this passage is all from an interview I conducted three days after the NYC Marathon.

I've tried to kind of change my thinking to go off how you feel, regardless of what [blood test results] look like. When I got my blood test [on October 17], it was right after I ran the half. That's when we did the 400s and the 800s and I felt fantastic. That was the day I was like, 'Oh wow, if you need me to rip sub 70 quarters I could have.' I felt good.

Then I believe that Saturday must have been my double. Leading into that, the only thing we changed a little when I spoke with Alan was my electrolyte intake because my sodium, potassium, and magnesium numbers were low so we were thinking that maybe that was the reason I was having some of my head symptoms. So I got this electrolyte mix and I tested it that day, on that workout morning, and I remember feeling good on that day but I had some bathroom problems. I basically barely finished the 2 x 6 because I had to go to the bathroom. And then the challenge of a day like that is eating and drinking a lot to recover from the morning and get ready for the afternoon. Because it was a 25-mile day. After the 10 x K, I went to the bathroom again and one thing I do remember, and I don't know if this is TMI or not, but there was some blood in my stool.[4] Was that the electrolyte mix having a little adverse effect on me, because it was kind of the first time that cycle where I felt like I had had some real stomach issues? Where if I look back to years ago, like the Chicago Marathon, I remember doing a workout in Camp Verde and I had that same feeling where my stomach just felt bad after.[5] So I did my best to recover and I thought I was at the right effort level that day. I definitely was in control. Obviously I was tired come the

---

[4] TMI = Too much information

[5] Steph ran the Chicago Marathon in the fall of 2019.

afternoon because it was a big workload. The next day actually felt pretty good, pretty decent, but then I would say starting Monday or Tuesday is when I started to feel a little like I was going downhill.

To tell you how I feel about hearing her say all of that is difficult. I am pragmatic and realistic to a fault. On one hand, I believe her 100 percent. More than 100 percent if that were possible. I don't doubt for a second that she is feeling this way. But on the other hand, I still have to wonder if stress isn't somehow involved. It is just difficult to understand why, over the years, she has run so well at 5k, 10k, and the half marathon and yet not performed to the same level in the marathon. It would be different if that was a pattern across our entire team, but if anything, it's the opposite. Our best performances have come in the marathon above all else. Of course, there have been races at shorter distances where she's felt these weird symptoms as well, but you can get away with a lot more in a race that takes 30 minutes versus a race that takes two-and-a-half hours. The marathon will expose your flaws.

The question now was could Steph, or maybe more appropriately Steph's body, be in a good place next Sunday? Though we didn't have any more big tests left to assess where she was at, we at least had a couple of sessions to watch her run fairly hard. If those went well, I wasn't going to be too concerned.

The first of those sessions was on Wednesday and we once again separated Steph and Aliphine. Before Boston in the spring, which had gone well and was one of the best two or three marathons of Steph's career, she had run a smooth 6 x 1 mile workout in this same spot on the schedule. So we stuck with what had worked before and assigned her the same workout.

Aliphine though, was still dealing with the worry that she hadn't done quite enough yet. As such, she had called me on Sunday to discuss what we were going to do this week. I was worried she was going to ask for more mileage than we normally do this week, or a longer final long run, but that wasn't the case. Evidently, I had already convinced her that there was nothing more we could do on that front. We had simply run out of time and she needed to pull back, freshen up, and build up the glycogen stores necessary to run well in NYC. What she did request, however, was a workout on Wednesday that would be more sustained. She didn't want repeats, she wanted that feeling of continuous running at marathon effort one more time. I understood that. And I have sort of a bank of different workouts that I've used for this session that occurs roughly 10 days out, depending on how the segment has gone. One of them is an 8-miler where you run the first four miles really smoothly at your marathon effort (no faster), and then pick it up a touch on the next four. In my experience, it has been a nice confidence builder—and that's what she needed. So that's what we did.

Steph's mile repeats went well on paper. She ran them all in almost exactly 5:25, as prescribed. She was pretty robotic in her execution that morning and let Alan, and Jenna, and I know afterward that there was a reason for it. She was about to get her period. She described the day:

I had the 6 x mile workout where I did it but it didn't feel awesome. But I also know I was PMS-ing. It was about five days before my cycle, and usually that's when I feel the worst. But I tried to stay really positive.

Alan, Jenna, and I were happy with the workout. And when Steph told us where she was at in her cycle, it made total sense that she didn't feel like a million bucks. Being honest about the effect that an athlete's cycle has on training is important and, thankfully, is much more commonplace these days. Though, to be fair, we still have a long way to go.

Aliphine had actually finished up her workout before Steph had started hers. Once again, we had to get out on Lake Mary early to beat the wind. And we didn't want to bug my friend Grant for a third time to come out and help so this time it was Allie's husband, Tim, that was assigned to bike duty. Which meant, by the way, that I was on baby duty. Tim and Allie's one-and-a-half-year-old daughter, Zoe, would have to ride in the back seat while I drove along. It was a family affair for sure. And to add to the Aliphine entourage, Mike McManus from HOKA rode along with me as well. Mike and his wife, Lora, bought a house in Flagstaff earlier in the year and the plan is to move into it full-time in two years when Lora's daughter graduates from high school. But for now, Mike just flies in here and there. I knew he was in town this week so I invited him to come out and watch the workout and he was more than happy to join.

If you are really nerding out on all of the training so far you might recognize that this session, 8 miles at marathon effort or slightly faster, is pretty much the same thing Aliphine did on Saturday for 15 miles. And maybe you're thinking, "What's the point of doing the same thing two workouts in a row?" And that would be a valid question. But remember what I said earlier, "With Aliphine you have to pick your battles."

The difference between Saturday and today would be the shoes. On Saturday, she didn't wear the super shoes. She wore a pair of prototype racing flats that did not have a carbon fiber plate. Today, she wore the HOKA Rocket X 2—the shoe that she wore this spring when she won the USATF 25k Championships and the BOLDERBoulder10k, and the shoe that she'll wear in NYC. It has all the bells and whistles—a carbon fiber plate, the latest and greatest geometric design, and the PEBA foam that has revolutionized the sport. Once again, we were rolling the dice a bit because if she didn't run faster than she did on Saturday we risked her wondering if the shoes were really as good as they were hyped up to be.

Fortunately, as has been the case going all the way back to the decision to move forward with training after the injury scare in early September, it all worked out. She ran the first four miles a little quick—closer to 5:30 than 5:35, and then her final four miles were all in the 5:20s. Overall, she ran under 44:00 for 8 miles on Lake Mary, the fastest she had ever covered the distance in training at 7,000ft. And perhaps best of all, she was finally tired afterward. It was almost like a peace came over her. She was ready. She knew it.

And now I didn't have to worry about her doing too much over these final 10 days. She was going to rest up and get ready to unleash her fitness in NYC.

STEPH'S TRAINING THIS WEEK:

Monday: AM – 6 mile easy run
PM – 5 mile easy run

Tuesday: AM – 8 mile easy run
PM – 5 mile easy run

Wednesday: 6 x 1-mile at half marathon effort with 2 minutes rest

Thursday: 9 mile easy run

Friday: AM – 8 mile easy run
PM – 5 mile easy run

Saturday: 14 mile medium long run

Sunday: 8 mile easy run

Total Weekly Mileage: 80 miles

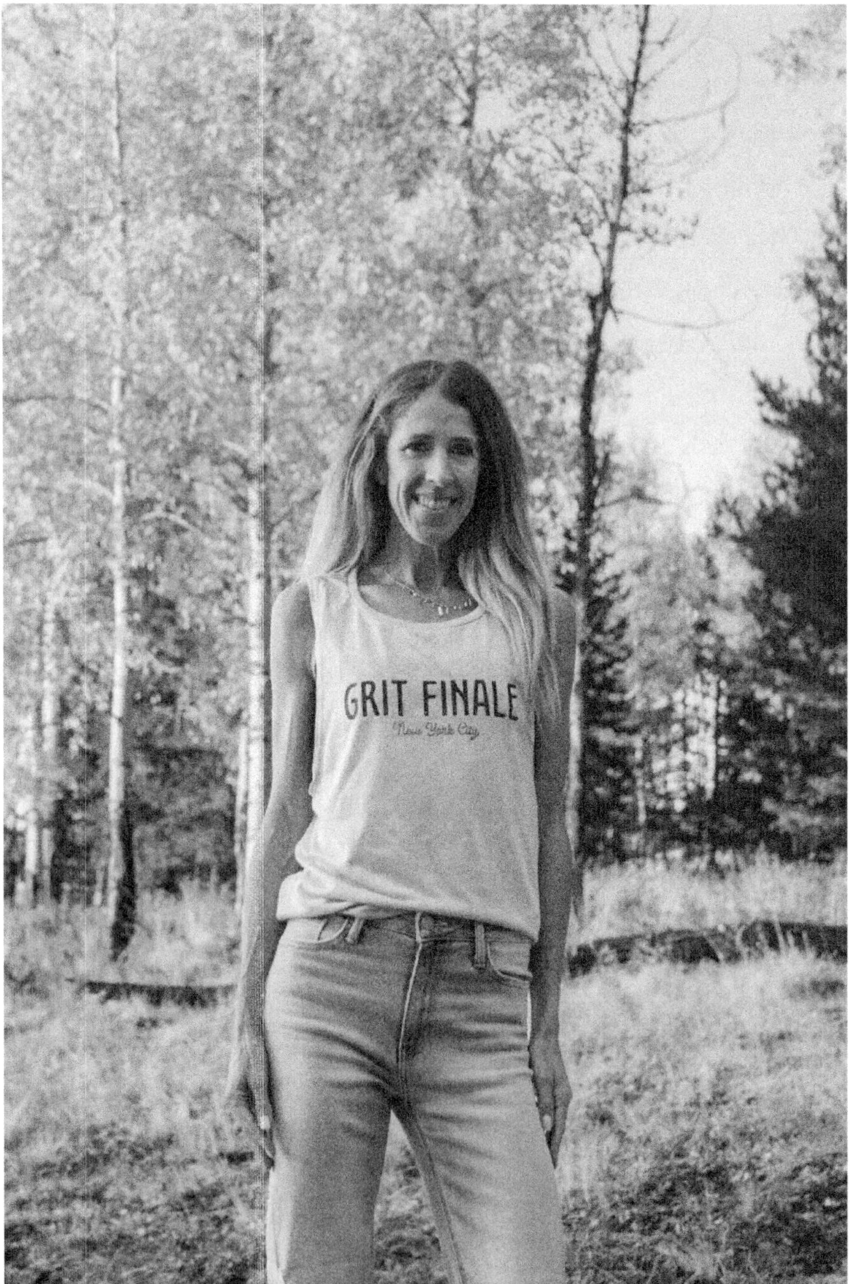
GRIT FINALE
New York City

CHAPTER 12.0

Grit Finale

1 WEEK OUT FROM THE NYC MARATHON.
OCTOBER 31ST – NOVEMBER 5TH

I can say with confidence that I was as excited one week out from NYC as I had been for any race since the Olympic Trials in 2020. Steph, Aliphine, and Matt were all healthy, and all three are proven prime-time players.[1] It was Steph's last marathon as a pro. Aliphine, in my opinion, had a real chance at the podium, and maybe even an outside chance to win if a few

---

[1] This is a sports term meaning they show up on the biggest stages.

things went our way. And we were finally going to be wearing super shoes after three full years of competing in marathons at a disadvantage.

My gut feeling about Steph was that she was going to have a good day. I was trying very hard to stay open-minded about what that could mean. But I had known since the professional women's field was released back in the summer that it would take one of the best performances of her career to finish in the top 10. It was just simple math. This was the deepest field I had seen since we've been coming to New York. I did believe that the weather, which had become the prevailing topic of conversation, was going to play to her strengths. The forecast was calling for temperatures at the start in the 60s, climbing into the 70s by the finish, and with 75% humidity. Steph has run well in the heat and humidity throughout her career, including as recently as August when she won the NACAC 10,000 on a brutally hot and humid night in the Bahamas. I knew she was confident about her ability to run well in those conditions.

I heard her say on more than one occasion during the week that no matter what, the weather wasn't going to be any worse than it was in the Bahamas.

Not necessarily to prepare for the heat, but we did go down to Camp Verde on Tuesday to do our final session at lower elevation. I have always liked to do that last workout down there if we can because it feels so gosh darn easy to them. We like to run 2 miles at marathon pace, 8 x 400 at 10k pace, and then finish up with 2 more miles at marathon pace. It was nice to have Steph, Aliphine, and Matt all together in one place for this one. For a variety of reasons, that hadn't happened much at all during this segment. As such, you could feel the energy with all three of them in one place.

I must confess I was happy that I was the one that got to go down and coach this workout. Alan was back with his family in Colorado and Jenna stayed up in Flagstaff to work with the young guns. Knowing that my coaching role will continue to diminish once Alan moves to Flag full-time, and once he's taken over Aliphine's workouts, it was not lost on me that this might be the last time I got to really be in charge of one of these final sessions. I relished the opportunity.

The session went smoothly, and I have to say that Matt, especially, looked good. I've come to use the word, champion, over the years to describe a certain type of athlete. A champion, in my mind, has an inherent belief in themself, looks forward to competition, and thrives during the very hardest part of a race. A champion doesn't let outside factors affect them. A champion sees virtually any unforeseen variable as an advantage. And a champion can go to a deep, dark place in terms of pain. Matt Baxter is a champion. I could not wait to see him race on Sunday.

Of course, Steph and Aliphine are champions as well, and the job of a coach becomes much easier bringing a group like this to a big race. As such, I wouldn't describe my mood as nervous. By mid-week, I'd just say I wanted to get this show on the road. Fortunately, NYC week is quite busy so time tends to fly by.

Aliphine, with Tim and Zoe by her side, flew out to New York on Wednesday because she had been invited to participate in the professional athlete press conference on Thursday. Steph wasn't asked, which felt like a bit of a slight, but I really didn't care since it meant she'd be able to fly out a day closer to the race. Given the choice, it's always my preference that we leave 2-3 days out for a domestic marathon if possible. The further out we have to leave, the longer we have to be away from our routine, the longer we're down from altitude, and the more time we have to spend in a stressful environment. Fortunately, Allie loves the energy in New York. She thrives on it. So if anyone was going to have to get to town early, I am glad it was her.

Matt, however, was a different story. Though, as referenced, he's a total champion, he's also an introvert from a small town in New Zealand. New Plymouth, where Matt grew up, has a population of 87,000. Flagstaff, where he's lived his entire adult life, comes in at just under 80,000. Manhattan alone is home to more than 1.6 million. Shoot, the New York City Marathon itself has 50,000 runners. Add to that the stress of traveling with his partner, Emily Roughan, and their two-year-old son, Miles, and there was just a touch of concern about how he'd handle everything.[2] As calm and confident as I was, a coach always finds something to worry about.

---

[2] Emily may want to kill me for including this but when they got to the airport on Thursday morning she realized she had forgotten her passport—not a good situation for an international traveler. It took a lot of wrangling but they were eventually allowed on the plane and Jen was able to go over to Matt and Emily's apartment and grab the passport before she flew out to New York herself. Major crisis averted on that one. Emily—at least I only put this in the footnotes!

I certainly wasn't worried about Steph's travel even though I am sure it was chaotic with Riley and Hudson. Steph and Ben have been traveling with the boys since they were infants. Confession; I never really understood why she insisted on bringing them to so many races when they were that young. I mean, they weren't ever going to remember. But now that they will, I suppose that all of the travel as little guys made them more used to things than they would have otherwise been. And Steph has dialed in how to ensure that they are well taken care of, and that so is she. Namely, they bring a babysitter. The sitter stays with the boys while Ben and Steph stay in a separate room. It's a smart setup. Again, she's a pro.

My own travel was more fun than normal because Jen and Addison were making the trip. They haven't come to too many races over the years. Travel is expensive for one thing, but it also takes them away from things that Addison has going on back home—namely her dance lessons. If any of you reading this are dance parents then you know the crazy level of commitment it takes to be part of a competitive studio. I must admit that in our family, Jen bears the brunt of the chauffeur duties…which I appreciate. And of course, Addison puts in all of the hard work. So for them to be able to get away from all of that for a weekend in New York City was pretty darn cool, and well deserved.

It worked out where I'd be able to spend Saturday and Sunday night with them as well, which was nice. Alan and I had a room together that was provided by the New York Road Runners, but then he sprung for his own room on Saturday and Sunday and flew his wife Shayne out as a 25th anniversary present. The bottom line was this whole weekend was going to be a family affair for everyone. And that just speaks to the importance of this race, and the confidence we all had that it was going to go well. You don't bring the spouse and kids if you think it's going to go poorly.

Friday is when things began to feel real. Alan went out for a run with Steph (and Ben) in Central Park where they discussed the final race plan. As had been the case since NACAC's in August, they seemed to be clicking well and so I didn't feel a need to get involved in any sort of race strategy discussion.

I ran with Ben and Alan and that was nice because the last workout had been on Tuesday so I think it was time to do something a little more up-tempo. 3 x 2 minutes was just a chance to get into race pace again. Alan and I, we talked about the weather of course. I wasn't being neurotic about it but it would have been naïve to not think it was going to be a factor. I just asked him if there was anything different I should do, or take into account, and he talked about the worse the conditions he thought the better for me because he thought I was able to handle things and make smart decisions. We kind of just reaffirmed everything we had been working on during the training cycle and my strengths as an athlete. I feel like we already had a plan but we really narrowed it down and dialed it in on that run.

I did find out from Alan that they also mutually agreed not to think of this as her last race so as not to put any extra pressure on her, or to put an importance on this race beyond what we normally would. Maybe it's the sports documentary fan in me, but I personally would've leaned into that. Whether it was John Elway winning his final Super Bowl, or Ted

Williams hitting a home run in his final at bat, or Kerri Strug, bad ankle and all, nailing her vault in the final rotation of the 1996 Olympics to give Team USA the victory, it just always seems like the true champions step up when they have to. When they have no other choice. When there is no tomorrow.

However, the pragmatic part of me knew that she was as fit as she was going to be and that she was going to make good decisions during the race, like she always had, regardless of whether or not she truly believed this would be her final marathon. The bottom line is the run went well, the chat went well, and she felt ready.

Matt was a different story. He hadn't gotten in until very late on Thursday and thus wanted to go for his run a little later than Steph. I happily volunteered to jog up to Central Park with him from the hotel, though I'd need to turn around soon thereafter to get back for a meeting. My schedule at the major marathons is always quite full—chatting with agents, marketing types, and various industry insiders. This particular meeting was an important one as Alan and I would be getting together with Mike McManus and his boss at HOKA, Steve Doolan. Having the chance to sit down with the decision makers, the people who sign the checks if you will, is an opportunity you don't say no to. So when I got Matt into the park and to a flat-ish spot where he could do the prescribed 3 x 2-minute pushes that were on his schedule for the day, I made sure to point out how to get back to the hotel—again this is someone used to Buffalo Park, not Central Park. I gave him a knuckle bump and took off. "Took off" is strong, though, as a strained calf courtesy of an ill-advised old-man track workout the previous week was really holding me back. I'll just admit it, I had to stop and walk. And I was late for the meeting. Damn it.

But that was the least of our problems. After the meeting that I was late for ended, I got a text from Emily. Matt still wasn't back from his run. This was a problem. Where the hell was he? Turns out, despite my best efforts, he had gotten lost on the way back to the hotel. Instead of going south toward the Hilton, he had headed due east toward First Avenue. He downplayed it because it probably only added on about a mile-and-a-half to his run, but we were concerned because it was a whole bunch of unnecessary stress and an extra hour or so on his feet when you consider all the stops. Alan and I decided right away that we'd have him sit out the scheduled panel discussion that evening at a local running store. Matt was more than okay with that.

The rest of us soldiered on though. Steph had a group run in her honor from the HOKA pop-up shop on 69th and Columbus at 4:00 pm. The route would form a giant "S" on the streets of Manhattan, something in the endurance sports world now known as "Strava Art."[3] Ben and Kellyn, who HOKA had flown in to make some brand ambassador appearances, led the run since Steph had already gotten in her workout earlier in the day. She merely shook some hands and kissed some babies when everyone

---

[3] Strava, if you don't know, is a website/app that serves as sort of a central library for athletes all over the globe to upload their GPS data. Individuals save their "activity" on the site and their "friends" are able to see it. That social media component of the site is what has turned it into a worldwide phenomenon. Strava promoted this run through their channels. They also provided raffle prizes for the post-run Q&A.

got back and then sat down inside the shop for a Q&A emceed by her good friend and former business partner, Lauren Fleshman. I had more time than normal in the weeks leading up to New York to work on brand activation surrounding the race and this was one of the events that we were pumped about. Getting Lauren and Picky Bars involved, along with Strava, at a HOKA event, was some great co-branding. I was able to get the Q&A started with some quick introductions before heading back to the hotel with Kellyn for our next event.

She and I, along with Alan, took the subway over to Brooklyn to speak at a local run-specialty shop—Brooklyn Running Company, about how to prepare for a marathon. Not to toot their horns too much but I'd say a free panel featuring a two-time Olympian and someone who has been eighth, seventh, and sixth at the NYC Marathon is a pretty solid value. The Brooklynites must have thought so too because the store was packed. I served as the emcee and just fed questions to Kellyn and Alan. They crushed it. The whole night was a blast and it took me back to my days as a running store owner when I had always loved events like these. To me, these sorts of things are what put the special in specialty. It was always my belief that if you built a community around your store, and you gave back to that community on a consistent basis, and in an authentic way, that people inside that community would almost feel guilty buying their shoes anywhere else. I could tell Brooklyn Running Company was that kind of store. I left there feeling really good about what we had just done, about my job, and about the race on Sunday. Plus, they gave me a free shirt.

A nightcap with Alan and one of our NAZ Elite board members, Bob Tusso, at a bar just down the street from the Hilton, polished off a successful day.

Saturday is typically a little easier than Friday as brands don't usually schedule any events for athletes or coaches to attend the day before the race. The same goes for the New York Road Runners. Aliphine had been at the presser on Thursday, and was one of the featured athletes at their opening ceremony on Friday night, but now her duties were done. Steph was going to make a super brief appearance just to say hello at the start of a Picky Bars group run in Central Park, but other than that she was free to relax. They each had a 3-mile shakeout run on their schedule which they knocked out, separately, in the morning. Aliphine, in particular, likes to do her last couple of runs solo on race weekend. It's a bit of a quirk, one of many, but one that I totally understand. When you've won as many races as Aliphine has, and you've done things a certain way in the days leading up to those races, you tend to want to stick to what you're used to. Of course, doing those runs alone is about the only thing that remains the same. Gosh only knows when she'll actually do the runs. I found out on Saturday that she had done Thursday and Friday's runs on the hotel treadmill at night because she had waited too long and it was dark out by the time she was ready to go. Crazy. But I suppose it's better to be so chill that you don't mind knocking out your run on the treadmill because the day got away from you, than so neurotic that you feel like you have to do it at some exact time, in some exact manner.

And those last runs aren't going to make much of a difference anyway, unless you were to stupidly do too much. In fact, Alan decided to have Matt take Saturday completely off. A little of that decision was due to him getting lost the day before, but more so it was because his knee was bothering him. To this point, I haven't even mentioned it, because to this point in the lead up to the race I hadn't thought much of it. He had fallen on a run about two weeks out and landed pretty hard on his right knee. There was a little bit of soreness in the immediate aftermath but nothing that seemed to hinder his running in any way. He had looked, and felt, great in that final workout earlier in the week and all systems were a go. However, and maybe it was the travel, but it bothered him on Friday to the point that he had to tell Alan about it. Fortunately, Alan is cool as a cucumber when it comes to things like that and he just told Matt to take the day off on Saturday and that he'd be fine on Sunday. I agreed. Adrenaline, after all, is a hell of a drug.

The one slightly stressful thing you do have to do as a pro marathoner on Saturday is prepare your race-day fluids. The race usually gives you a window of time in the afternoon to drop off your bottles and so it's on you to mix them like you've practiced, decorate them so you can seem them on the table, and label them properly so the bottle you want at each particular station will be where you want it to be on race day. I joined Matt and Aliphine in the pro athlete lounge as they did all of the above on Saturday afternoon. It's fun to see an athlete go through this process for the first time. It's nerve-racking even for the most seasoned of veterans, but for a debutant, it can be downright frightening. I thought Matt was handling it well, all things considered. The whole reason I was up there though, was because Aliphine had finally reached out via text to talk about the race. I knew we needed to have a chat, but I was hoping she'd be the one to initiate it, seeing as I knew that would mean she was ready for it. Plus, we hadn't really had our race talk about the Trials until the day before either, so there was a little superstition involved as well. Coaches can be quirky too I suppose.

So when she was done filling and decorating her bottles, the two of us headed down to the lower level in the hotel to the ballroom where we were to label them, check them in, and drop them off. We ended up being there the same time as Scott Fauble, one of the athletes that had left our team in December of 2021. I had worked with Scott from the summer of 2015 all the way through the end of '21 and we had a tremendous amount of success. We even wrote a book together in 2017 called *Inside A Marathon*, that documented Scott's training for that year's New York City Marathon. It was not fun when he left. It hurt. But as I said in an earlier chapter, it ended up working out for the best, for him and for NAZ Elite. Sometimes people need change. He and I have gotten through all of that so it wasn't weird at all to see him. In fact, it was fun to chat as he and Aliphine labeled their bottles. Allie took us through her intricate, and let's just say unconventional, plan to tape two gels to some of her bottles so she could take one and stuff the other into her sports bra "for later." Faubs had a good laugh at that one. It was like old times.

Once her bottles were out of her hands and fully checked in, we found a lounge seat in the hallway with no one else around and had the race chat. I had prepared what I wanted to say in my head but didn't want to be too scripted. Above all, I wanted to be calm and confident. That's always the number one thing as a coach in these situations, in my opinion. After all, how can you expect the athlete to be calm and confident if the person that is supposed to be guiding them is nervous and insecure.

I let her go first. She talked about the weather. At this point, as I said earlier, it was pretty clear that temps would be in the upper 60s and that there would be a fair bit of humidity. I assured her that it was an advantage for her. She's raced well in those exact conditions, or worse, many times throughout her career, and the science suggests that the number one way to acclimate for such a scenario is to make sure you are sweating on your runs in the two weeks leading up to the race. That wasn't a problem for Aliphine. She overdresses on pretty much every run she does anyway, so she sweats year-round. She felt good about that. Box checked. On to the next topic; strategy.

I have been watching the New York City Marathon since I was a kid. I can vividly remember sitting on the floor in my parent's bedroom watching the race on ABC on a Sunday morning even before I had become a runner myself. It always fascinated me. It still does. And one of the main reasons is the course. Yes, it's unique because it traverses all five boroughs, but for me, what makes it so gosh darn interesting is that it is constantly forcing you to think. This isn't Chicago, or London, or Berlin where you lock into a pace and try to stay there for 26.2 miles. This is ups and downs, bridges, potholes, headwinds, tailwinds. And for the professional athletes in the lead pack, it's just one constant stream of decisions. There are surges, slow-downs, surprise contenders, silly moves early that you have to ignore, hard moves late that you have to cover, and that's on top of what every marathoner has to battle internally—all of the demons inside your head yelling at you, even screaming at you, to slow down, to say no to these tough questions, to avoid the pain.

But to try and prepare mentally for every possible scenario seems a fool's errand to me. That's the whole point of getting fit. And that's essentially what I told Allie. We didn't do that before the Trials, we didn't do that before the 25k Champs, or before BOLDERBoulder. And all of those went pretty darn well. What we did was believe in her decision-making, and believe in her fitness. Which brought us to our final point of discussion; just exactly how fit was she?

I said, "Let me put it to you this way, even if the weather were perfect, and it was going to be a really fast day, I believe you'd have a chance to be on the podium."

That was what she needed to hear. And that was what I truly believed. The chat ended. She took a deep breath. I gave her a pat on the back. And off we went.

The last time I saw the crew was a couple of hours later at what's called the technical meeting. Every major road race has one. All of the athletes and coaches gather in a ballroom in the host hotel and the race director, or the professional athlete coordinator, takes you through all of the logistics for the next day. In the case of the New York City Marathon, Sam Grotewold is that guy.[4] The first thing Sam always does is thank everyone for choosing to run New York, noting that there are plenty of great options out there. He's right. Between Amsterdam, and Chicago, and Berlin, and Valencia, and the list goes on, the fall is full of big city marathons. He then thanks his co-workers at the Road Runners. This year he announced that Kerin Hempel would be stepping down from her role as CEO. We all gave Kerin a round of applause. Then he asked race director Ted Metellus to come up and speak. Ted is awesome. His words were full of energy and excitement and set the perfect tone. The meeting had a very positive, and very professional feel.

Of course, then Sam had to get down to business. He took us through a PowerPoint presentation that started with the weather. Then we looked at the timeline for the morning. Seeing that breakfast opens at 4am is always a reminder that you're not going to get a whole lot of sleep. My favorite part is what comes next, Sam going through the entire course, highlighting each borough, each bridge, and of course Central Park. You can feel the nervous tension in the room. It's always complete silence, out of respect for Sam, yes, but also because you know every single athlete in that room is getting a giant lump in their throat as the realization hits that this thing is happening. They are going to run the NYC Marathon. I loved it.

After the meeting, the athletes got their official race bibs and our crew met up in the hallway to say our goodbyes for the evening. Aliphine, Matt, and Steph were all in great spirits. We took a picture with the three of them

---

[4] Sam is the professional athlete coordinator for the New York Road Runners. He does a tremendous job and has the respect of the entire industry.

and said we'd see them in the morning. For Alan and I, it was out of our hands at this point. For the athletes, the hope is that they have come to peace with their fitness, and with their race plan, and that they are relaxed.

I looked at the training cycle, and I knew as far as split-wise I had run a lot of 5:25s to 5:35s in training. I knew I could do that in the race. It would just be a matter of where that was going to be with what the front pack was doing. In years past, I've had different race plans where I was like, 'Alright I want to be with the lead pack but if they start running x, y, z that's too fast and I have to check off.' I did that in almost every New York, and almost every Boston, and sometimes it worked out and sometimes it didn't. I think going into this race I was like, 'You know what, I keep doing the same thing and it's not yielding a better result so I want to try something different.' It was kind of like I'm in the lead pack and I want to finish on the podium so that's the place that I belong.

STEPH'S TRAINING THIS WEEK:

Monday: AM – 8 mile easy run
PM – 4 mile easy run

Tuesday: AM – 2 miles at marathon effort. 8 x 400 at 10k effort. 2 miles at marathon effort
PM – 3 mile easy run

Wednesday: 7 mile easy run

Thursday: 7 mile easy run

Friday: 3 x 2 minutes at marathon effort with 1-minute jog recovery

Saturday: 3 miles

Sunday: TCS NYC Marathon

Total Weekly Mileage: 75 miles

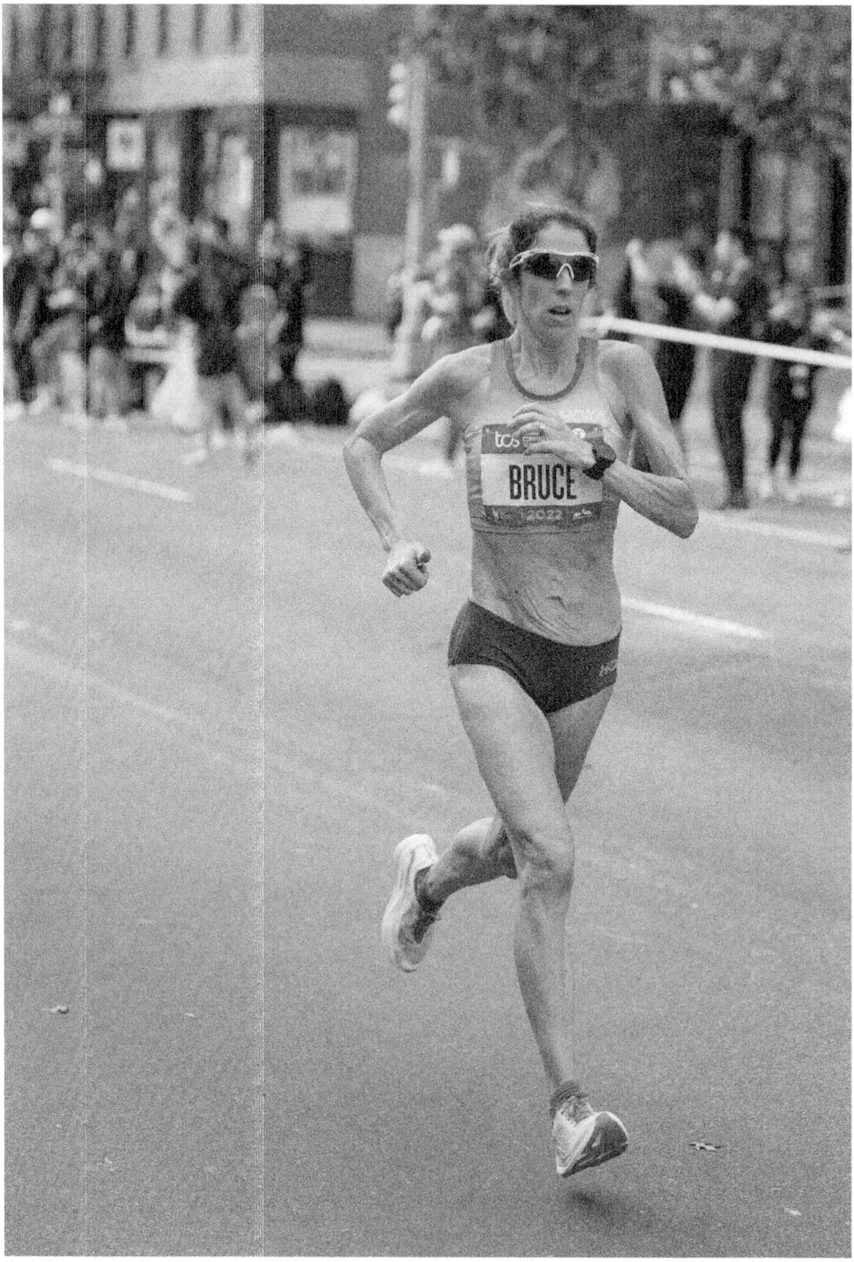
BRUCE
2022

CHAPTER 13.0

The Race

THE NYC MARATHON. NOVEMBER 6TH

This is your moment. Your time. I know you are nervous but what a privilege to be nervous. Something matters. It's on the line. Your story isn't written. Your dream is still there for the taking. You will doubt a few times in the race but be confident. Be the bad bitch you are. Channel all the love, all the support, all the stubbornness it took to keep going. Mom and Dad are with you. Like mom said, "You can run one step further." Get on that podium. Why not me. Let's go Steph, I'm proud of you. – Steph

That was the note Steph wrote to herself one hour before the start of the NYC Marathon. By that time the athletes had been dropped off at Ocean Breeze Indoor Track Facility on Staten Island—the staging area for all of the pros. These were her final thoughts before taking off for a light warmup jog, even lighter than normal on this particular day because of the above-average temperatures. A seven or eight minute jog is really all you need on a day like this. Adrenaline will take care of the rest. And as you could hear from her own words, Steph was chalk full of it.

Meanwhile, I was back in the hotel with Jen and Addison. They were just waking up when Steph, Matt, and Aliphine were going through their warmup routines. I had been up since 4 a.m. when I snuck out of the room as quietly as possible to go down and have some breakfast before meeting up with the athletes to see them off. The hotel lobby on race morning is sort of eerie. It's still dark outside, closer to the middle of the night, than the morning, really. The coaches and agents arrive first, milling about and making small talk with one another with one eye on whatever conversation they're having, and one eye on the elevators, anxiously awaiting their athlete/client to appear.

Not surprisingly for us, Matt came down first. Being his first marathon, being the biggest race he's ever been a part of, you kind of figured he'd be bright and early. Alan and I decided to go ahead and walk him over to the buses that were parked outside. No need to stand around in a lobby full of nerves and tension. As we walked out the revolving doors of the Hilton, I did notice one thing right away. There was no chill in the air. This is my seventh time at the New York City Marathon and the first time it wasn't cold at 5:30 a.m. As if I didn't know it already, the weather was going to be a factor.

As we started to walk back toward the hotel, Steph and Ben were walking toward us. Again, predictable. Not so much that Steph was antsy, but more so that Aliphine is always one of the last athletes to board the bus. More on that in a second. Steph was smiling ear to ear. She loves this stuff. She's never one to have a "game face." Even if she tried, I don't think she could hide the happiness she feels on race morning. There is a reason she's still doing this at 38 years old. And of course, Ben's the same. Most human beings look a little tired at 5:30 in the morning. Not Ben Bruce. The guy oozes energy 24 hours a day. It was great to see them together, the perfect couple, side by side, in a place, and on a day, they both love so much.

We hadn't said much to Matt, and we didn't say much to Steph either. What's there to say really? The fitness is what it is at this point. The race plan has been agreed upon. Now it's just a "good luck" or a "go get 'em" and you send them on their way. And then you wait.

Speaking of waiting, it was another few minutes before Aliphine finally strolled up. It's hard to put into words, but she has a unique gait on race morning, or when she gets out of the car on a hard workout day, or when she's walking up to a podium. It's a confident, bouncy, happy stride. Some might call it a strut. And it's just so Aliphine. Like Steph, she thrives on the big stage. It's why New York is the ideal race for her. While the noise, and hubbub, and energy of the city drains many athletes over the course of the weekend, Allie seems to absorb it and use it to her advantage. She was ready to go. I could feel it.

When the buses take off, all us coaches, agents, and spouses head back to our rooms. In years past, I've spent a good chunk of the couple of hours we have before the race starts, going for a run on the Westside Highway bike path, along the Hudson River, and just kind of releasing some of that nervous energy that's inherently present on race morning. Unfortunately, with my bum calf, on this morning I just had to go back and try to get some sleep. Which didn't happen.

When Jen and Addison finally woke up and got situated, we went for a walk over to Dunkin' Donuts for some breakfast. It took a bit longer than we expected, and we barely made it back to the room in time for the start of the race. I kind of liked it though. Now the worst part—the waiting—was over. It was game on.

I felt the heat and humidity early on but then when I look back and I hear other people and they were like, "I knew at mile 8 it was over." I didn't feel that so I think I made the right decision. I didn't necessarily think, 'Oh my gosh this is too aggressive.' There were even some moments when Des [Linden]...I love her...'cause I just know the move she's going to make. She took off going up the bridge and I feel like I matched that more than other people and I was at the front because I was thinking, 'If she goes aggressive then we have to run faster splits to catch her.' That was the fastest split we had ever run [on the first mile].

I think we ran 5:43 up the hill.[1] That might be a record. The fastest I had run up that was 6:10. I think what Des knew was two things; she knows how to run her own race, and we did have a tailwind going north. I think she was like, 'I'm going to capitalize on that.' What was nice about that was we eventually caught her and then going downhill I think we were like 5:23. I was thinking, 'This is exactly what we want to do,' and it was a huge pack. I knew it would be a lot of women. I thought going in that there were 20+ women who had run 2:26 or better. That's a really deep field.

While Steph was matching Des's moves, and processing, in real time, how the race was shaping up, the rest of us were watching it all unfold on TV. Very early in the race, ESPN showed a pre-produced piece on Steph and how this was her final marathon as a professional athlete. They talked about her congenital heart defect, her family, her history here in New York. They showed pictures of Steph back in Flagstaff, and with her mom in her final days. Geez. Thanks a lot ESPN. It was definitely one of those, "I'm not crying, you're crying" kind of moments.

Emotions aside, I felt like we got off to a good start. The one tiny worry about the women's race I had was whether or not Ethiopia's Gotytom Gebreslase would take off from the gun like she had at the World Championships just three-and-a-half months earlier. On that day, in Eugene, Oregon, Gebreslase set a torrid pace early and never relented, eventually winning in a Championship record, 2:18:11. If she tried that today it would force us to make some tough decisions early, much earlier

---

[1] The first mile of the race is a monster uphill as the runners climb the Verrazano Narrows Bridge.

than I would have preferred, and then it becomes a different sort of race. The sort of race Steph referenced that she's had to run before where you're simply trying to run a certain pace and pick people off late. For lack of a better term, a race that's just not as fun. Going in I felt pretty strongly that no one would do that though, because of the nature of the New York course, and because of the weather. I was right as it related to the women's race. The men's race was a different deal.

The first split that shows up when you're tracking the leaders on the NYC Marathon app is 5k. When I saw that the main lead men hit that mark in 15:00 I was pretty surprised. That's 2:06:35 marathon pace. These guys were not going to run 2:06 on this course, on this day. It just wasn't possible. The good news for us was that Matt was never going to try and run with the lead pack today anyway. Though I may have admitted above that it's not as fun, sometimes you have to forego what you want to do, and be pragmatic. Someday soon, maybe even in his next one, Matt will be able to try and win a marathon. Today was about learning the event, having a good experience, and beating as many people as he could. A nonsensical early pace from the leaders was actually a good thing for Matt Baxter.

Meanwhile, Steph continued to run and assess, run and assess.

One thing I think I did really well is there were surges every time going into the elite fluid stations, and I know the Kenyans and Ethiopians do that for whatever reason. And I never got caught up in it. I was like, 'I'm table 10, I'm going to let them surge,' and then after a quarter mile I was back in the lead pack. So I feel like I didn't make any unnecessary moves. Then, when Des made another move, I don't know, somewhere past 10k, I remember looking up and being like, 'Oh shit, she's kind of far ahead.' In years past that's when the pack then had to run pretty fast splits to catch her. So I remember feeling like we settled and then I actually went to the front and I started to try and close the gap. It felt appropriate. I think I ran a 5:30. That seemed totally fine. Once I did that, though, I remember feeling Hellen Obiri and Aliphine.[2] Then they caught me and they started bridging the gap. I feel like that was the smartest thing I could've done. After Aliphine went to the front that's when it was like, 'Okay, now it's on.'

Sitting in my room, watching Steph, and then Aliphine, make sure the pack didn't let Des get away was certainly a point of pride. You do what you can as a coach, and a program, to try and prepare your athletes for a race, and part of that prep is to watch video, is to understand our opponents, and how races are run. I don't think either Steph or Allie necessarily thought Des was going to get away and win the race, à la Meb Keflezighi at the 2014 Boston Marathon, but they both knew that if they let her get too big of a lead, the pack would eventually have to drop a really fast mile or two to catch back up—the kind of move that could have put them in trouble. It was much easier to run a 5:30 now, than a 5:10 later.

Alan and I were texting back and forth as things got going. After Aliphine caught up to Des he sent the following:

---

[2] Hellen Obiri was one of the pre-race favorites. A two-time World Champion at 5,000 meters and a two-time Olympic Silver Medalist, NYC was her debut marathon, but she was still considered someone who could win it all.

She must feel good, made up that gap quickly.

Meanwhile, the men's race got even crazier as Brazil's Daniel Do Nascimento continued to keep his foot on the gas pedal, hitting the 10k mark in 28:42 and halfway in 61:22. For reference, the NYC Marathon course record is 2:05:06, set in 2011 by all-time great Geoffrey Mutai on an absolutely beautiful crisp, fall day. Do Nascimento was on pace to run just under 2:03:00 on a day that was anything but. It was almost cringeworthy to watch, knowing the carnage that was surely to follow. The more sensible players came through halfway fast as well, in 1:03:35. This thing was going to be a fight for survival over the last 13.1 miles. Matt came through in 1:06:40, very close to what we had discussed beforehand, though to be slightly critical, he had not gotten there in the most efficient way. Each of his 5k splits to this point had been slower than the one before. Still, he's Matt and I knew he would keep grinding.

Steph would get to that point as well.

I think there might have been nine to eleven women in the lead pack come eight, nine, ten miles in. And then it kind of gets blurry after that. The point of the race [where it got tough] was going up the bridge. When we went up the Queensboro Bridge I was like, 'I can't keep running this pace.' It was just kind of natural. But I think one thing I've always been good at is even though I fell off I'm going to keep running hard. Then from the top of the hill, 25k, I would say I was alone from then on.

Watching the splits come through and seeing that the women hit halfway in 1:12:17 was what I expected, but if you would have given me some truth serum, I would have had to tell you that deep down I knew it was too fast for Steph. Remember a couple of weeks ago I told her that 2:24 was going to be an aggressive pace for her. Not unrealistic, but aggressive. Of course, on this day, given the weather, it probably was unrealistic to believe she could maintain that pace for the entire race. However, I was at peace with it. This was her final marathon. I wanted her to have this type of experience—running with the leaders until you can no longer physically keep up. She had earned the right to try. Plus, she wasn't the only one who had employed this strategy. And I liked her chances to fight for every inch of those last ten-plus miles.

And our chances for a special day were far from over. Aliphine was right in the thick of it. Coming off the Queensboro Bridge and onto First Avenue, she was right there, in a pack of eight, and she looked great. In fact, at the elite fluids station just past 25k you could see her take a gel and stuff it in her sports bra…for later—just like she planned it. Lonah Salpeter was doing much of the leading with Gebreslase and Obiri on her shoulder. Salpeter, a naturalized citizen of Israel, had won the bronze medal at the World Championships in July and seemed eager to keep the pace hot. Viola Cheptoo, the NYC runner-up in 2021, was also there. As was

University of Kansas alum, and our fellow Flagstaff resident, Sharon Lokedi.[3]

Steph was a ways back, and all alone.

On the bridge I remember thinking my right quad was kind of going, but I was just trying to push off to get power off of it. Then I went down the big hill and you make the sweeping turn to get onto First Avenue, and that's when the electricity of the city comes back. But I've been really able to tune out all that noise even though there was all this cheering. I knew that some of my friends and family were supposed to be there, but I didn't see or hear anyone. I was just in the zone. On First Avenue though, is where I felt the first big dip in energy, physically. That's when I tried to not look at my watch. I just told myself to keep running steady.

Not to compare watching a marathon to running one, but there's always a little dip in your own energy as a coach when your athlete falls off the lead pack. That chance for a home run kind of day is what keeps your heart rate up, keeps you buzzing, when you're watching it all play out. When Steph fell off I felt for her, but again, I knew from the day the fields came out that it was going to be really difficult for her to finish in the top 10. And that was still a possibility so I stayed positive. Same for Matt. In fact, top 10 was going to be even harder for him, given that this was his debut, and

---

[3] Sharon competes for the Under Armour Dark Sky Distance team, based in Flagstaff. Like Aliphine, she came over to the U.S. for college and stayed here after she graduated. She still competes for Kenya, however, and spent much of the training block for NYC in Kenya.

that his segment had been a little rocky. When I saw that he crossed the timing mat at 20 miles, still averaging 5:10 per mile (2:15 pace), I was ecstatic…for two reasons. One was simply that he had gotten to 20 miles and, more than likely, he was going to finish. Having not even run the day before with a sore knee, that was no guarantee going in. And second, he was going to finish pretty darn high. The majority of the men in the field had gone out over their heads. The early leader, Do Nascimento, was literally lying on the ground in pain…unable to even continue running. The two Americans that were getting a lot of pre-race hype, Olympic medalist Galen Rupp and Olympian Shadrack Kipchirchir, had fallen way back. Rupp dropped out of the race at 16 miles. Kipchirchir would eventually jog home in 2:28:15. More and more it was looking like we were going to have three races we could be really proud of.

Steph was employing all the mental tricks necessary to keep one's head in the game.

As we made our way up First Ave I remember Nell Rojas passed me.[4] And then Emma Bates came by me.[5] It's difficult. And it's difficult because you can always say should I have stayed back with them, but again I feel like, 'No. That's what I've done every other year.' At Boston I did that and I never caught Nell. I also know, at that point, we're still only 17 miles in and a lot can happen. I could turn it around. Or they could have gone too early. You just don't know. One

---

[4] Steph had beaten Nell back in September at the USATF 10k Championships. Nell had beaten Steph earlier in the year at the Boston Marathon.

[5] At the 2020 Olympic Trials, Steph finished sixth and Emma was seventh. At the 2018 USATF Marathon Championships, Emma won and Steph was second.

thing I've always been able to do in the marathon is believe that it's not over until it's over. So even though it's difficult when they're passing me, I've been there before and I've come back on people. So I just tried to keep getting to every mile, but I had a really bad patch from when we got off First Avenue going into The Bronx. From there to 22 it was really, really rough.

I don't know if on this day I ever really let myself believe Aliphine was going to win the race. Much like I tell the athletes, it's dangerous to go into a race with that as the goal, or at least as the only goal. First of all, what place you finish is never completely up to you. Sometimes, your competitors are just better. Given her fitness, my hope was simply that she give herself a chance. That she make good decisions throughout, so as to finish as high as possible. It was exactly what I told her when we had our pre-race chat. I'm nothing if not honest.

All the way to the 30k mark, she was executing the race as well as you could possibly hope. She was relaxed. She made a couple of moves when she felt she needed to, like catching up to Des just past 10k, but for the most part she stayed in the pack and did very little. She was running like the veteran that she is. At 27k, though, it was decision time. Gebreslase, Obiri, and Cheptoo, moved hard. Aliphine did not seem concerned. She stayed relaxed with the other four athletes, and just like that, a pack that had been eight was now three. However, it wasn't over. Far from it. During the 20th mile of the race two of the athletes from the second pack, Lokedi and Salpeter, began to bridge the gap. What had been an 11-second lead at 30k (18.6 miles) was now down to five seconds just two kilometers later. Aliphine, who was right next to the two chasers at 30k, did not join them in their pursuit. And while her decision to stay relaxed at 27k was a good one, this time she missed her chance. The lead pack was five now and she was 24 seconds back. The podium places were getting away. Like Steph, she would have to find a way, mentally, to grind away over the last few miles.

But unlike Steph, Allie was alone the entire last 10k. Steph, fortunately, eventually found herself in a battle with Gerda Steyn of South Africa.

I remember having that wobbly feeling and having thoughts like, 'Oh my gosh I'm not going to make it to the finish.' That was 20 or 21. You're fighting your body, because your mind is saying, 'Go,' and your body is saying, 'No.' I don't know if it knows if you push any harder you will fall over. It's this weird feeling. But it's so hard when you look back you think, 'Oh was I not running hard enough?' But you feel like you are in the moment. I remember when we started the climb on Fifth Avenue, I was just like, 'Push into the ground.' And then I feel like I was moving quicker, but you don't know if you are or not. They said we were supposed to have a headwind, but I didn't feel it as much. So I thought, 'Okay this is good.' But I also remember thinking, 'Gosh I am going so slow.' But no one was passing me. And that was telling me, 'You're still fighting, you're not giving up.' And maybe other people are giving up. When we got into Central Park, that's when Gerda caught me. I loved her because we had talked a little before the race and I remember she raced with Aliphine in 2019. She was the one that Aliphine was in a battle with, and I think she beat Aliphine. But as soon as she caught me, I don't know how to explain it—whether it was my brain, or my body—but I remember you [Coach Ben] in 2021 when I was running with

Grace, you said, 'Win this race.'[6] And that's all I remember thinking. I didn't know what place I was in, but I was like, 'Stephanie you need to win this race.' So then I switched over and tried to be in a 10k. Just go. And I sold out that next mile. It caught up to me I think because when we hit 25 it felt like she moved away from me very quickly, even though I feel like I was running hard. But I would say she helped me get to the finish line faster than I would've gotten there myself.

Soon after I watched Steph go by in Central Park, battling with Gerda, I got a call from Ben. He was emotional. I suppose you would even say a little angry—angry that Steph had been so aggressive early on. Philosophically he believes in a more conservative, even-paced approach to racing. He's a professional pacer for pete's sake so you can't blame him. He thought a really high place would have been there for the taking if she'd have gone out smoothly in 1:13:00 or even 1:14:00. But I just reminded him that this wasn't our choice. This was her final marathon, and it was her call. She owed it to herself to try. Plus, to be fair to her competitors, almost everyone else she was up against went for it, just like she did. In the end, only two athletes that beat Steph had come through halfway in 1:13:00 or slower—Jessica Stenson of Australia who finished ninth in 2:27:27, and Gerda who finished 12th in 2:30:22. Steph was 13th in 2:30:34, her fastest time ever on the New York City course.

As Alan and I made our way from the 24-mile mark and cut through the middle of Central Park over to the finish, we were already happy with the

---

[6] Grace Kahura of Kenya was ninth and Steph was tenth at the 2021 NYC Marathon.

day, thrilled even. We had cheered as Aliphine had gone by, firmly in seventh, and then for Steph as she battled for 13th.[7] We had screamed at the tops of our lungs as Matt came by stride for stride with 2016 U.S. Olympian Jared Ward.[8] When you don't know if an athlete's going to be able to finish the race when the darn thing starts, and then he's racing an Olympian two-plus hours later, you can't be anything but thrilled, really. We chatted in between breaths, running as fast as we could, desperate to see the crew.

All three of them were already in the post-race tent by the time we finally made it. Steph had already reunited with Ben and the boys and was laying on the ground, completely exhausted.

I honestly didn't have many feelings right away. I don't know if it was just being so fatigued, maybe I was numb to it. I have been through that so many times. So yeah, I just didn't have any. But what I did a really good job of, going into this, was I was not very emotionally charged. I was really looking at this as any other marathon. And I don't think it got to me, or it was overwhelming in any way. Especially that finish. I wasn't going through this, 'Oh my gosh this is it,' kind of thing. I was just like, 'Get to the finish.' Once I crossed the line and I see my

---

[7] Aliphine did indeed finish seventh in a time of 2:26:18 (her personal best). She was the top American finisher by 35 seconds over Emma Bates, who finished eighth.

[8] Jared finished 11th and Matt was 12th. They both spoke fondly of the battle over those last few miles, Jared getting the best of Matt on the downhills, and Matt pushing the ups. There aren't two nicer guys in the sport than Jared Ward and Matt Baxter.

people I think my first thought, always, and I don't know if this is bad or good or whatever, I'm always saying, 'Was this enough?' To them. And that's probably because I know how much time and energy I took from everyone leading into this race so I just want to ask them, 'Was this enough for you guys,' because I know it is my career, and it's what's important to me, but I couldn't do any of this without anyone else.

We hung around that tent for a long time. It's weird. In a way you know you need to get out of there and get everyone back to the hotel so they can recover. But somewhere in the back of your mind you know that when you do, then that's it. This incredible journey, these last four months of hard work—or in Steph's case—these last 15 years, is over.

We made sure that wasn't it though, at least for this one day, and into the night. Steph and Ben had worked with Steph's management team—Josh and Carrie Cox, and Larry Rosenblatt, to set up a retirement party later that evening. It was held at the swanky Dear Irving on the Hudson rooftop bar. Steph was absolutely beaming the entire time. It was cool to see so many of her competitors, and so many running industry bigwigs, show up to honor her. Des Linden was there. I saw Emily Sisson and congratulated her on her still fresh American Record.[9] Mike Smith was in the house with his wife Rachel, someone Steph has become good friends with over the years. Jack Fleming, the new President and CEO of the Boston Athletic Association was there, along with Mary Kate Shea, the BAA professional athlete recruiting director. Five-time Olympian Abdi Abdirahman was in

---

[9] Emily set the new record, 2:18:29, at the 2022 Bank of America Chicago Marathon on October 9, 2022.

attendance, along with his girlfriend Diane Nukuri—another one of Steph's longtime competitors and friends. Even the great Meb Keflezeghi was there. Meb took a picture that night with Abdi and Alan—the three had produced many a great battle back in the late 90s and early 2000s when they were on top of the U.S. running world.

It was just a total blast. Larry, who had really put the night together, said a few words. Ben spoke as well, and he did an awesome job, because he spoke from the heart. He talked about his parents, and both Steph's late parents, and about all the friends he and Steph had made in the running community along the way. And he cried. A lot. And it was pretty damn special.

I had the honor of speaking as well. I didn't have any notes so I can't recall exactly what I said but I know I focused on two words—gratitude and belief. I said thank you to Steph for believing in what Jen and I were building way back in 2014. Thank you for believing in me as a coach. And thank you for believing in this whole crazy transition—bringing in a new head coach, Alan, in the eleventh hour of her career. I told everyone there that it said a lot about Steph, about her loyalty, her character, and her integrity, that she was so open and understanding during this process. But mostly I talked about her belief in herself. Because coaches, and training, and workouts…are a little bit overrated. They're important of course, but they mean nothing without an athlete's belief in oneself. And we were all there that night because Steph believed in herself like no one I've ever met. A 5:00 miler in high school, and a good college runner but not great, Steph believed there was more. Not hoped, not wished…believed. She believed enough to move to Eugene, Oregon, and eventually Flagstaff, Ariz. She believed even after she found out she had celiac disease. She believed even after having a baby, and then another. Hell, she even believed after finding out her heart wasn't as strong as it was supposed to be. She is an amazing human being and I was so proud to be able to stand there that night and tell everyone listening how much I admired and respected her. It was the most meaningful speech I'd ever given.

Looking back, I wish we would have given Steph the mic that night to talk to the crowd herself, but I think we just wanted her to enjoy it. To drink as much wine as she could handle and to listen to us talk about how much she meant to all of us. But still, I regretted that. So in our final interview for this book, a month-and-a-half after New York, I asked her what she would have said.

First of all, I'm glad I didn't get the mic that night. [Laughing] For one I was drinking a lot. But also I always feel like I'm the one talking so I did like that it was you guys. The whole night to me was about gratitude. So when I was thinking about throwing the party and inviting people, it was going all the way back to 2007 in my mind. Thinking about my post-collegiate career starting, and who were the people that have been pivotal along the way. One person in particular, he works for Hawi Management now, John Hricay. He was one of the people that said, 'I know you're from New York. I see potential, and a future, in you.' And then he got me a New York Athletic Club sponsorship. So I might've told little stories like that, stories like 'You believed in me when no one else did and there was no reason to.' And [the NYAC sponsorship] wasn't a lot. It was something like $300 to $500 a month but that was enough to offset rent and *then I could babysit less. So yeah, I just had people along the way that did little random acts of kindness that sort of told me, 'Hey, you're making the right decision to want to try and pursue this.'*

Then I probably would've singled out Mike McManus, and maybe said that, 'Hey I know I came to the group when I had another sponsor [Oiselle] but you okayed it and that made a huge impact because it meant I could keep running with Coach Ben and the team.'

And I would've talked about Josh [Cox] who had to negotiate for me during some awkward times; he negotiated through my pregnancy, back when that wasn't happening a lot in the industry. He was amazing through all of it. And of course Larry [Rosenblatt] for all his planning of the party, and assisting me in those few weeks leading up to NYC. He has been a great friend and sounding board for me.

And I would've given my Grit and Growth girl gang a shout. I've been friends with some of them since college, and some since high school, and some only recently the last couple of years. They made the trip out just to watch me in this last New York. Two particular people, Tianna [Madison] and Dawn [Harper-Nelson]—it was so cool to have them there because they've been at the highest level in the sport of track and field, like winning Gold Medals, and I haven't even come close to that.[10] *They walked into the Hilton lobby race weekend and*

---

[10] For the record, Tianna Madison has three Olympic gold medals: the 2012 4 x 100-meter relay, the 2016 4 x 100-meter relay, and the 2016 Long Jump. Dawn Harper-Nelson won the gold medal in the 100-meter hurdles at the 2008 Games in Beijing.

they were like, 'Oh…this is what running should be like.' Because they used to go to huge track meets, like the Diamond League, and this was just a different feel. They were almost like, 'I want to be a marathoner.'

Lotti [Bildrici] was there. Lotti was someone who came in and revamped my diet and nutrition approach and I think that made a huge impact on me almost making the Olympic team in 2020 in Atlanta.

Then my "home-away-from-home" family, the Creegans. Kevin is who married Ben and I, and they've always been my family that we get to go stay with when we visit Long Island.

And of course Lauren [Fleshman] and Jesse [Thomas]. I think Lauren and Jesse, what we experienced last year was a dream come true; selling Picky Bars. But for me it was two things. It was the best month of my life I guess you could say, in May. And then my Mom died in June and that was the worst month of my life. It was amazing how life can throw these two totally different things at you. On one hand, Wow, I just made the most money I've ever made and then the next month I would have given it all back if it meant my mom didn't die. So for Lauren and Jesse it was similar in a way where we were so proud of what we'd achieved over the last decade, but it did kind of feel like we were giving away our child. The bottom line is I would've thanked them for being two people who were like, 'Who is this crazy girl with this dream?' She thinks she can make an Olympic team. She's only run 33:30 [for 10k in college]. But they never laughed at me. They never thought my dreams were too big, or too bold. And that's one of the reasons we actually started the company. They had the brains, and the *business sense, but if I hadn't pushed and said, 'We can do this,' maybe it wouldn't have ever started.*

With Ben, he and I had joked when we were planning the party that this was a big year for us. 2022 was our ten-year anniversary. So I would've said to him, 'Thanks for planning our anniversary party.' I would've thanked him for being such a selfless person. What is required in this sport takes a lot of selfishness and it's particularly hard as a woman, and as a mom, to know that the whole family revolves around my schedule. And for many years it has been that way for us, ever since Ben transitioned away from his own professional running career. I would've said to him that I hope it's been worth it, and I hope the sacrifices he's had to make for us, and for the kids, even though I didn't achieve all of the results I was looking for, I hope it was all worth it. And I know he would've told me back, 'It's always worth it, because it's with you.'

So I think I just would've thanked everyone for being part of my journey. Because even though I don't get to thank people every day, I don't get to see all these people every day, this was a chance to have my whole life in one room. I just would've thanked them all and said, 'Please enjoy the open bar.'

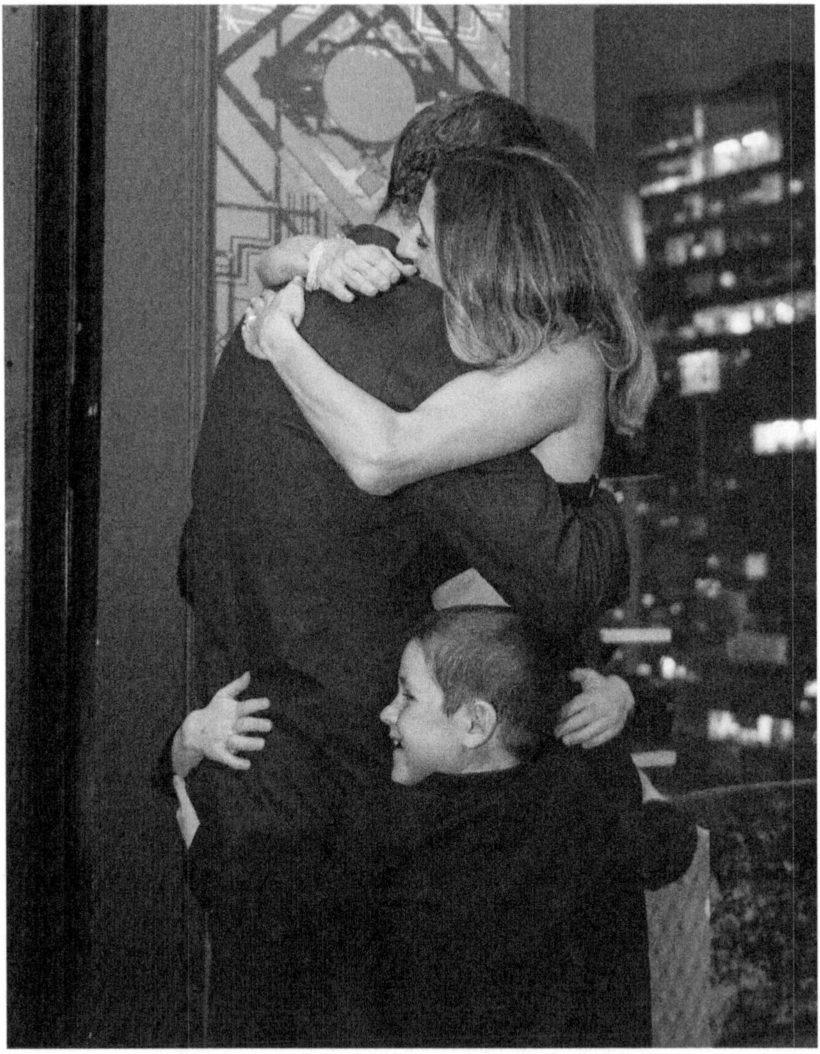

EPILOGUE

The Decision

NOVEMBER 7TH – DECEMBER 22ND

It's hard to explain and I guess I don't know if I'll ever have an explanation, or I guess I don't think I need to have it, because I was just dealing with a lot at the end of the year [2021]. And I thought that I had to have a, 'This is what I'm doing.' And then I got to a point where actually it's okay if I change my mind and I don't have to apologize for changing my mind. - Steph

Welp, we got some big news from Steph one day after we got back from New York. She's not retiring!

I was not shocked. Writing this book, hearing the little hints she dropped along the way, and just knowing Steph like I do, I sensed this was coming. I sensed that she no longer wanted to retire. She sent Alan, Jenna, and myself an email on Tuesday, November 8 that laid out what she wanted to do. It was a two-year plan which means she wants to compete until she's 40, nearly 41 actually.[1] That email set off a series of events that included Steph's agent, Josh Cox, reaching out to Mike McManus from HOKA to ensure that the brand would be willing to exercise a renewal on her contract that would take her through the end of 2024. They were of course. They'd have been crazy not to. Regardless of what Steph does "between the curbs" between now and then she will no doubt remain one of the most popular distance runners in the United States. Her fans are loyal, they're passionate, and they are going to be following Steph long after she finally does retire, whenever that may be.

And of course, that's her choice. Hers and Ben's. As it should be. But that doesn't mean it will be easy for everyone else to understand. It wasn't easy for me. In fact, I was kind of a jerk about it. I had really fallen in love with this story, this idea that she was going to go out on top instead of waiting until her body failed her. I loved that the year had gone so well, that she had won the NACAC title, and the USATF 10k Champs. That she had run one of her best marathons ever, if not her very best, in Boston. Even New York, which wasn't everything she wanted from a performance standpoint, was an incredible weekend, punctuated by a retirement party for the ages. I loved that she would now be able to focus on adding to her

---

[1] Steph was born on January 14, 1984.

family, if fate allowed, and then begin honing in on any one of the many business ventures she and Ben have started over these last few years. As someone whose best memories, and proudest moments, have come after my running days were behind me, I was excited for Steph to experience this next chapter of her life—a chapter that I know she's going to crush.

So, in the name of interviewing her for this very epilogue, I asked her to meet for a chat on December 22, a full six weeks after that email. We met at the brand new HOKA NAZ Elite Performance Center—a 2,600 square foot facility overlooking downtown Flagstaff. The center is still being built out as I finish up the writing of this book, but will eventually house our own weight room, sauna, treadmill, podcast studio, and more. It was not lost on me during the meeting that affording this space may not have even been possible without the contributions Steph has made to our program. Not only have her results elevated our standing in the running world, but her commitment to building her personal brand, and our team's brand, has increased our value to our current sponsors, and to any future sponsors as well. She is a part of the very fabric of NAZ Elite.

But what should have been a really fun hour talking about all of the cool experiences she's going to no doubt have during these next two years, I really dug into why she wasn't retiring. I grilled her basically. I thought whatever was going on in her head was the new story; an inside look into an athlete contemplating retirement. We never get this as fans. Why did Michael Jordan come back and play for the Wizards? What went on behind the scenes with Tom Brady's retirement and un-retirement thirty days later. And what's Serena Williams going to do? Has she really played her last match?

So I asked Steph what changed in the 48 hours between her retirement party and sending that email? What happened to not wanting to be one of those athletes that waited until their body broke down to retire? Did she feel like she was honest with her fans during this process? And the list went on. At the time, in addition to how good I thought these in-depth questions would be for the book, I thought they were coming from a place of love. Sort of like a parent who's worried about their child's risky career choice. It's not that the parent doesn't want their child to succeed, it's that they're afraid they might fail. And then they'll be hurt. And you never want to see someone you care about get hurt. I do believe that was part of it. To make sure Steph understood that this year was really special and that absolutely nothing is guaranteed, moving forward. Father time is undefeated, as they say, and at some point she is going to have to move on.

In the most pragmatic sense, I wasn't wrong. But I learned something from her answers, and from a discussion we had the next day when she let me know she was not pleased with the questions, that brought clarity, and I suppose finality to this entire project.

Steph didn't move to tiny little Eugene, Oregon in 2007, after an okay-but-not-great college career because it made practical sense. Or because anyone else on the face of the earth thought she should.

She didn't start an energy food company, in her 20s, from scratch, with two of her best friends, because math tells you that's a good idea. After all, only 25% of small businesses make it 15 years or more.

She didn't decide to start a family in 2013 because that was going to be a good decision for her running career. Pregnancy and labor wreak havoc on a woman's body. That's just the totally unfair truth of nature.

She didn't become a founding member of NAZ Elite in 2014 because joining a brand new team, and a brand new coach, at 31 years old, is a proven recipe for success.

She didn't think about the negative consequences sure to come her way via pea-brained internet trolls when she shared pictures of her postpartum stomach in 2014, diastasis recti and all. She just wanted to help fellow moms.

She didn't create her racing schedule based on money, or legacy. She always chose based on the experience she believed she'd have. And the relationships she'd built with certain events.

She didn't give up when she found out she had a congenital heart defect. She sought out the best sports cardiologist in the country who confirmed that she was 100% okay to continue running at a high level.

When she announced to the world that she was going to retire at the end of 2022, she didn't do it to draw attention to herself. She did it to share what she truly believed would be the final leg of her athletic journey with her fans.

And now she's changed her mind, and that's okay. Like MJ, and Brady, and Serena, athletes don't owe us an explanation for every single thing they choose to do. And even if they wanted to tell us, oftentimes, they wouldn't be able to, because so many of these decisions aren't calculated. These extraordinary human beings don't operate like the rest of us. They don't fear negative consequences. They don't consider worst case scenarios. And they sure as hell don't concern themselves with the opinions of others.

So even though I asked Steph all those hard-hitting questions, thinking I would force her to reveal the thinking behind her decision, I eventually had to ask myself, "What was the point of all that…what did I learn?" Well, I learned something really valuable. Something that makes me excited for these next two years. Something that leads me to believe maybe, just maybe, she can defy the odds a few more times and produce something, like she's done so many times before, that others did not believe was possible.

I learned that Steph Bruce doesn't make decisions with her head. She follows her heart. And it's all worked out pretty damn well so far.

Printed in Great Britain
by Amazon